SELECTED POEMS

Poetry collections by Herbert Lomas

Chimpanzees are Blameless Creatures
Who Needs Money?
Private and Confidential
Public Footpath
Fire in the Garden
Letters in the Dark
Trouble

Translations by Herbert Lomas

Territorial Song: Finnish Prose and Poetry
Contemporary Finnish Poetry
Wings of Hope and Daring *by Eira Stenberg*
Black and Red *by Ilpo Tiihonen*
Narcissus in Winter *by Risto Ahti*
The Year of the Hare *by Arto Paasilinna*

SELECTED POEMS

Herbert Lomas

SINCLAIR-STEVENSON

First published in Great Britain in 1995
by Sinclair-Stevenson
an imprint of Reed International Books Ltd
Michelin House, 81 Fulham Road, London SW3 6RB
and Auckland, Melbourne, Singapore and Toronto

Copyright © 1995 by Herbert Lomas

The right of Herbert Lomas to be identified as author
of this work has been asserted by him in accordance with the
Copyright, Designs and Patents Act 1988.

A CIP catalogue record for this book
is available at the British Library

ISBN 1 85619 613 5
Typeset by Deltatype Ltd, Ellesmere Port, Cheshire
Printed and bound in Great Britain
by Cox & Wyman Ltd, Reading, Berks.

In memoriam
Mary Lomas 1940–1994

My first, best and last reader

Was stürbe dem Tod
als was uns stört,
was Tristan wehrt
Isolde immer zu lieben,
ewig ihr nur zu leben?

ACKNOWLEDGEMENTS

The poems in this selection were originally published by the following: *Chimpanzees are Blameless Creatures* – Mandarin Books, 1969; *Who Needs Money?* – Blond & Briggs, 1972; *Private and Confidential* – London Magazine Editions, 1974; *Public Footpath* – Anvil Press, 1981; *Fire in the Garden* – Oxford University Press, 1984; *Letters in the Dark* – Oxford University Press, 1986; *Trouble* – Sinclair-Stevenson, 1992.

Many of these poems have also appeared in *Ambit*, *Encounter*, *The Honest Ulsterman*, *The Hudson Review*, *London Magazine*, *New Spokes*, *Poetry Durham*, *Poetry Review*, *P.N. Review* and *The Spectator*.

Thanks are due to all these editors and publishers.

A NOTE TO THE READER

At first you may not like what you see here, but if you read on you may find other things. Critics have accused me of being both lightweight and heavily obscure, justifiably in both cases, and the problem is which of me to foreground. In the end I decided to forget about critics and try to help a sympathetic reader to enter my work. As for the poems left out, I've not disowned them, particularly the ones in *Trouble*, still in print. Some are and some may well be better than these.

Yet a poet knows better than anyone else the shortcomings of his own work. My fault is that there's too much irony in my poetry. I was born sincere but life has taught me obliqueness. People, I know, want poetry that comes straight from the heart. And, in spite of everything, I'm here, exposed.

Both palaver and content are subject to time and place, and some of my times and places have been like separate lives. When I came back to England in December 1965, after thirteen years in Finland and very few visits home, I found England transmogrified. I abandoned all I'd written till then and made a fresh start. Since then I've made several fresh starts. I've also made some changes. As Valéry said, a poem is never finished, only abandoned.

Herbert Lomas

CONTENTS

Faustus Speaks

I

NOTES ON WITTGENSTEIN

What does it mean to say 'I hear'?
The piano, the air, the ear, the player?

What does it mean to say 'I hope'?
Is hope a feeling? How long can I hope you come?

And what does it mean to say 'I love'?
Your skin, your boots, your smell, your world?

No one says 'No. That wasn't true pain.
True pain wouldn't have faded – or faded so quickly.'

Is it you I love or myself?
And are roses red in the dark?

THROUGH THE NEEDLES

There are nightglows on a lake whose name I can't remember:
July midnight, in the north, the verandah of a broken hut.
In the daytime I saw the veins on a fly's dead wing.
I looked at the lake and dived in, as if it were a woman's body.
It received me with cold kisses and dashed cortisone
round my veins. Later she received me with hot kisses
and she was hot and gushing inside. All I can see now
are bright stained reds and peacockblues and an unveiled look
in her eyes she never had at any other time. She was made for love
and nothing else. I can only see her through pine boles and needles
but at odd moments feeling can seem as roomy as the planet.

DOWN THE HILL

A curtain of dusty sunlight in the street.
I walk through it and down the hill
from Exchange Station to the Kardomah caff.
Sheila Banks still
in my heart inhales the steam: somewhat –
with her cup clasped – like a squirrel with a nut.

She looks at me across the rim and smiles,
yielding and secret, failed nun,
ex-schizophrenic, cured consumptive,
who held my hand for fun
one afternoon at the pictures, and gave a bang
to my surprised heart, since I was young.

She tried to make me a Catholic, taking advantage
of what she'd done. Suffering was exquisite,
sent as a grace, she said, so felt no guilt
for giving me so much of it;
and fell in love with my friend and followed him
meek-eyed, eager to gratify every whim.

He didn't care for her and thought her rather
daft, could mimic her quite well,
enjoyed his victory over me,
was flattered by our little triple hell.
Pain was a shame to share, for he was vexed
by only loving his own sex.

We were a little crocodile from Chekhov: he
impassioned for a blond unaware
medical student about to be married,
I in love with her,
and she with him: I don't know where
they are now – and know too well to care.

Here's all the delivery of that blaze
without the flame: a little pain
new suffering has raised,
exquisitely sought out again.
Will they too go on living if we meet
behind the curtain of dusty sunlight in the street?

THE BYWAYS OF DESIRE

1.
Who can remember Haworth churchyard,
cocked stones, November wet,
the scratch of your match, the flame,
your cigarette end red –

the gravestone beneath us, drizzled,
as we lay under night with the dead,
and those arctic sheets in the Guest House,
your pineapple eyes, yellow with carnality,

smoked or drowsing, suffering love
dredged to your pupils – and two lines
toused in one cheek that said pleasure –
but love or what it brought or might

who can remember
or what you were like inside?

2.
It irritated your sister, driving,
that we lay in the back seat kissing.
Occasionally I saw her toss of head,
and anyway the back of her glowering.

Were we even in love? You needed relief,
a man again after your husband gone,
I to find out about love. I needed
flesh and wanted to touch it.

There'd been the blow on the spine one night
as I faced the burn in your eyes and knew it was on.
Then you looked down with a nod. But it'd been
a warning: you couldn't be rejected.

Recognition and pain: we'd be together for a while,
as if in love, and then need to be destroyed.

YE SHALL BE AS GODS, KNOWING GOOD AND EVIL

This apple that she gave to you
wasn't sweet flesh or vegetable dew.

If Othello was fiction, Iago too,
Shakespeare's *Othello* is no less true.

It wasn't knowledge that made you sin
but double knowledge, two doors to come in.

Good and evil, devil's fiction,
split the world in every direction.

The way out's the way in.
The flaming sword's in your brain.

TRUE LOVE

In the dark scented air
of coal dust and cat piss
two infant lovers stare
and shyly kiss.

No denser human bliss
can ever come to birth
on the dung and primrose earth
than this.

Later brutal kisses
and adult sweaty heats
will cheat them out of this
in laundered sheets.

EPITAPH

These two lovers were married a lifetime together,
fought for each other, fought against each other,
coped with poverty, unemployment and wealth,
betrayed each other in sickness and in health,
educated their children, then lived apart,
old irreconcilable folk, with angina of the heart,
in separate flats, in the same town, same part,
and died within an hour of one another.

OTHER LIFE

She was a burning glass.
A little sun inside had passed
through her from a hotter source.

And yet she was opaque.
Made from a childhood ache
that dark as particles could flame and shake.

She was dark, dark
and almost out of sight: a watermark
pressed in the paper of her book.

The book was all she'd been,
child, mother, slut, queen,
and all she'd ever done or seen.

If he'd read her,
he'd have learned to dread her,
certainly never dared to kiss her or bed her.

FIRST KISSES

The best kisses are the first.
First mother's kisses, and after that
the kisses in the Botanical Gardens
stolen among flowers.

Then there are the kisses when
you think you'll never be kissed again.

Kisses in foreign cities:
perhaps in a flat, perhaps in a rainy street,
panting because illicit.

And then, late at night, comforting
someone in tears. Perhaps it's because
she's so hot with suffering, or hasn't
used her kissing mouth for almost years.
But probably not: she just has a talent
and like so many talents, it's
been buried.
                                    Like her breasts
with their talent for being looked at and
looking back, it's a hidden address.

Not for everyday visit or caress.

HOW I LOVE MY SISTER

My sister was never born.
She came out of the horn
of plenty and back through the horn.

All my life I've been unexpectedly drawn
to my sister, who was never born.
You could say I've missed her.

Even as a tot I slipped my hand
up her skirt, a search not planned
but urgent for her tender hand.

I also adored her and didn't dare
to touch her dazzling skin or face her stare
that watched me from some little girl's hair.

She was very close to God and is,
and so I'm dumb as I come to her school
and will always behave like a fool.

I think she's my twin,
and she's often led me into sin.
But I've had to let her escape

back to her city of crape.
Friendship's perhaps the most
I can hope from her blonde ghost

if I want her to be a happy one,
and dark girls lead me on.

WHO

Made from her flesh
my flesh pricks
if she smarts.
Let the wind go near her bones
and my bones go cold.
If she groans in her sleep,
groans walk through the darkness,
and climb in with me.
Much that she's said
and left unsaid
is said in my head –
though I'd disown it.
And who am I
being myself alone
while I groan in the body of another?

AT THE CAMDEN ARTS

Since she's seventeen, and I'm, let's say,
much older, and, moreover, happily married,
which only makes me love women more,
and the girl's in love with the poet in the orange shirt
this evening, it's much wiser to say goodbye,
after getting five kisses of excuse, which I value,
and get on the tube at Finchley Road,
feeling, Well, at least, I've been treated considerately.

It's not very dignified leaving her to the younger poet
and going home to someone you love more, especially as you
would be allowed to if you wanted. But it does make
                                        something clear.
There's nothing now, nothing at all, to stop you
seeing that what you love's not veins, fingers,
rings and feet, but only these when you've got into
the esoteric hinterlands that these are the merchandise of.
It's not enough to fuck someone on a sofa one night.

Even these intelligent recondite women aren't unknowable
                                        enough for me.
It's you I'm curious about. Now I've landed on your coasts,
it's your rivers I want to explore, your inhabitants to trade
                                        with.
I'm entranced by your silences and cries. It's your customs
I want to study and bring your artefacts home to my
                                        museums.
There's a religion I can learn, I think, if I learn your
                                        language.
It hasn't a theology perhaps, but in its rituals I'll find, I
                                        suspect,
the sorcerous genitalia of all theology.

14

IMAGINATION

When I look at you, Mary, my eyes
are flickered on by a
shower of particles that
pierce my lens, tap

on my retina, wash
electromagnetic
currents up the threads of

my nerves to something that looks like a
cauliflower and weighs
three pounds. All the rest, love,
in fact the lot,

is pure imagination. When an
atom of sodium
meets a wild atom of
chlorine and they

synthesize into salt,
who imagines green gas
and white powder? I, love,

creator of brain, nerves, lens,
suddenly forget them
when I look at you
and create you

accurately as you are
at your imagined
far speculated you.

SENT

At Proprietary Perfumes they know as much as possible:
in their mind's nose a woman's lavishing herself
with plangent-smelling goodies, sending herself
glaucous: the man's incidental.

It's cheering her up. (Sales in fragrance products
actually boom in recessions.) After the ritual cleansing
a touch of perfume's an improving odour, exciting
the female with castorum, musk, civet and other glands.

Dabbing herself she feels pampered, erotically done-to,
voluptuously touched-up and *it* . . . She already feels
someone's after her. She's even attracting herself.

Though it's a strong garter of class, a sash of taste,
an aromatic affidavit of money, and a rumour of age-group
and experience, any man's perfume given to a woman's
a sexual innuendo, surely – like a woman's whisper to herself.

NEW SOURCES OF SEX

But now there's your body, and it still needs discovery,
                                        thank God.

Who dreams of what it'll be like in heaven? No splitting, but
fusion of the bodies, the combustion of angels in brilliant sex:
inexhaustible supply: five hundred times the burning
of all the world's fossil fuel in the graze of a hand?

Solar energy, wind potency, pushing of the tides, deuterium
                                        igniting . . . but
we're all ruined. As long as we dream of heaven it doesn't exist.
When all the petrol's burnt and all our children dead
faces with beautiful genes'll walk the prairies of light; yes –

but now? Still beyond your unmanageable hills
the unimaginable looks out and doesn't look out.
Unbeatable, impenetrable, wavering, lust like my own
is staring back from alarmed indoctrinated eyes.

I love you. And in spite of, because of it, I want
to colonize you: greed wants, this same inherited
greed wants to make new markets, exploit your
raw materials, open the interior, kill the Indians.

Discovery uncovers you: your musk, length of leg, brown discs,
shifting persona, I can rifle them, but you're a safe
with no back. The closer I burgle you the more your
                                                    contents vanish.
I'm a physicist in an atom, disappearing and opening out.

PERSEUS AND ANDROMEDA

The girl's quite free and naked and only seems chained:
in fact she's completely available and wondering what
the fuss is all about. The dragon looks like a Victorian
bicycle and is in fact a gimcrack mechanism in the man's own
                                                            mind.
Yet it's real enough: the teeth could needle through
to the bone and may do. The eyes' bestial killing fury
is a trained anguish in the man's own spine.
This is the terror that love is wound round.

He's the man with the sword. He pushes its neck aside,
but his eyes are meditative, not on its head or eyes,
but some hallucination of a Satanic God in his own insides.
Blue is the armour, icy blue, cold leaves, quite dead.
If he looked on a maidenhead, with the hair around,
the snakes would turn him to stone. Split by that split
he turns Medusa's face on the world to destroy it.
His power is the split mirrored in the fearful shield.

MUSK

Musk seemed to whisper hoarsely, a hoarse sound,
           with a throaty burr
going right back to the deer's gland,
to the muskiest scent snuffed out by the females
              and passed on in the rank glands,
                  a single grain of musk
perfuming millions of cubic feet of air,
           teaching sexwise nostrils,

Empress Josephine's musk, impregnating lace,
           inflaming Bonaparte's
antlered passion, impregnating her walls,
a musky perfume aphrodisiac for years
              in kings, queens, rajahs, sybarites,
                courtesans, drifting on particles,
navigating down the animal odour so maddening to
           the soft meat of feminine deer.

THE SIZE OF THE SEA

The size of the sea can make you sick with passion:
                 there's so much of it not used up –
much more than anyone can fit into a marriage
                 however much they love their husbands,
                 unless they're spiritual athletes.

People say the illusions you experience in love
                 are illusions. The visions of temples on the astral,
the seashores where you run in slow motion
                 with your beloved, her hair rising and falling
                 like a horse in a slow film,

the erotic pillared porticoes opening on a lakeshore
                 and purple water, where you find her lying
naked, one knee raised and lean over her, breathing,
                 a blue shadow. The belief that it'll
                 begin again another morning

after you're both dead, the wish to die,
                 to find those shores of orgasm, to see
the crystal eyes of the beloved as God imagined them,
                 to touch her celestial body and turn
                 literal flame,

to walk floating the plains of beautiful light
                 and the jewelled cities, drinking
unknown wine in heavenly cafés. There are some who say
                 reality's only a fish and chip lunch,
                 bills unpaid, and the children obstreperous,

yet you've only to smell the sea to smell that illusion's
                reality: those acres of sperm smell
are unusable up: the floating suffering it gives you
                as you watch it creaming and creaming in
                will make you leap in again and again

for lives you haven't lived and are going to live.

A HISTORY OF ENGLISH MUSIC
FROM BYRD TO CAGE

Every year now if I don't watch out
I'll catch him saying the same things.
Here he is with the same girl
and another face. It ends the same:

'They only want to be pregnant.
We should get into them in the morning
with a hard fuck and then talk about it
in the evening with our friends.

'It's as if I'm living someone else's life.
I don't like my work. I only do it
to keep her house going. She doesn't
get up till nine o'clock.

'I've made my own breakfast. At
nine o'clock at night
she's going to bed again. She
doesn't read or *do* anything.

'When my dad died my blood pressure
went up from a man of thirty-five's
to a man of sixty's.
It just shot up like that.

'My doctor implies I should leave her.
How can I expect to get rid of these
headaches and this bad leg?
The worst is I don't care a twat.'

23

And I? If I'm not careful I'll tell him
the same things: 'You're looking
somewhere else for the same fuck.
You're writing the same book

over and over again.' What frightens me
is that others will see in me
what I see in him: the same recorded performance
ground all over my flat surface.

He's bought himself a watch that
only registers time, lighting up red,
when he presses a button.
It costs him two pounds a year.

It'd be worth a few pounds
to buy another that gave us
a minute of forgetfulness
each time we pressed the button.

GROVES OF ACADEME

1.
She's not as young as she used to be – she
never was. Age's always trodden on her heel,
tickled her ear: twenty, twenty-one,
thirty, thirty-nine, forty? And always, always,
wasn't there? there was something, something
she could have done. In those days
a girl didn't ring or write to a man
as they can now and say they love him
or just want sex. Why can't she now?
She's old. She was young then.
What is she missing? She's got
a husband, a job, a beautiful child.
But beyond all that, something's
still unsatisfied, afraid. Is infinity
waiting for her? It's that infinity
in her now that wants to make her
take a man again. Infinity knows
her life's not yet begun. She'll never
have enough of life to fill infinity up . . .

2.
And afternoon's a hot time for ticking essays.
Heat shimmers on the Library wall across.
A face sits behind a typewriter at its
open window. Occasionally eyes meet.

Her glasses have grease on. A straggle of hair
hangs over an eye. She nibbles her lip.
These thoughts have come out of my lectures.
How depressing. She'd like a kiss – or highbrow talk.

It comes to her that what she wants is
something in her body – but for her mind
new knowledge. Someone's eyes are shining –
they'd open her and she'd be a person she's not.

Her legs are hot. Caressingly her hand rests there
and moves to the top. Does she know she's doing it?
She squeezes it tight and warm, folding it in, concentrating.
There's a man alone, down the corridor, working too.

But neither'll ever restore the other's body,
except in lucid dreams, where they've sometimes met at night.
Now she goes to the loo and fills a glass with water,
she tosses her hair and drinks it, tapping her foot.

CHANSON TRISTE

The leaves on the lawn under the chestnut
are suddenly shocking
like something squandered.

His aching head
will rest in summer moonlight's lap
and the poems he'll read
will make her *Primavera*
high summer and autumn all at once.

In her melancholy eyes
he'll drink so many kisses
so many caresses
he might even be cured.

Or is he drinking with so much pleasure
the old illness
through the new kisses?

A piano made out of water
and clouds
and sunlight
is taking a golden glamour
into its greyness.

For years
one can rely on
an imaginary love.

THE GHOST OF A ROSE

He was conceived by the Landscape of the Summer Solstice,
gestated in the National Film Theatre
and delivered one night, rather late
after something to drink and inner debate.

He'd a year to live. He knew he was dying
in the B Minor Mass and the walk back
past the Film Theatre, with bells
against a livid sky in a John Martin Hell.

Death came as the car stopped.
He cut off her stiff upper lip
and she cried at last on his shoulder, and he
cried without letting her see.

Life after death was three days
and then in agony the second death.
He'll watch her operation from
the touch lines – mixed hockey – and cheer her on.

He'll take an interest
in her score and escape
to the new landscape,
exploring his immortality.

TROUBLE

*'I will be no trouble to you. I sleep all day,
go to the theatre in the evening, and at night
you may do what you will with me.'*
– Marie Duplessis to Liszt

That summer's lakeside cabin makes me sigh:
that manic horse, too, with its madhouse eye –
in love with you. As was I.

As we trailed to the farm for milk, he ran like my heart
thudding across the field: nose over gate;
and once – did he vault it? – out in the night,

he'd nibbled your drawers on the line. Ass!
An edge of dissolved-in-saliva grass
greened the last shreds of your silkiness.

When I cracked a window, at your wish
I rowed and sprinkled the splinters: a dish
for the water sprite – and we never lacked for fish.

The ancient pike I caught's huge jagged
crocodile snout scowled, as it rose and wagged.
And now your hatred, even, that's almost flagged.

INVISIBLE MAN

Always she slept with
no clothes on: couldn't bear
pyjamas or a nightie.

I felt ethereal.
'I've a body, I've a soul,' I said,
'but I *am* a spirit.'

'So who's the Invisible Man,' she said,
'the ghost in the machine?
Is this the Middle Ages?'

'You smell me, you taste me,' I said,
'you suffer my kisses,
feel me inside you,

'think you know me,
but you don't see me.
Only I can feel me inside me.'

'You *are* a body,'
she said. 'You're afraid of it,
getting away from your corpse' –

turning her back on me,
wriggling close and pressing
her cold bottom against my belly.

SHINGLE STREET

Someone lying on the deserted beach
appears to be lying on someone else.
She lowers her head
and drinks him slowly,
holding him by the ears.

He's completely not-there,
and she, with her black hair
is a bee-sucker
after nectar
under his grey hair.
They must know I'm coming,
but they don't care.

It must be illicit,
nowhere else to go,
not going to be stopped
by my possible stare.

Rules are overnice
in Paradise.
Though no one marries
or gives in marriage,
their bright ice,
great seers say,
melts in the solar flare
of their fusion and confusion.
That's how they feel each other there.

Who doesn't wish them well?
Perhaps we too
in some afterlife
will find some angel

to give us fugitive love
when ordinary women no longer find us
worth the worry of.

REMEMBERING ADLESTROP

I too remember Adlestrop –
that compatible weekend in the car
when all the birds of Gloucestershire
seemed intoxicated by tar

and dawdled on the road. I slowed
to let them loop away. 'Adlestrop
must be somewhere here,' I said.
Then, towards dusk, a sudden stop.

A signpost: 'Adlestrop!' I cried,
not really having looked, and turned.
No railway: just the station sign,
yellow, conserved, and I somehow yearned

and grieved as a blackbird sang.
Had I an inkling even then that now
I'd hear it with wringing pain,
knowing your love had stopped, not how?

LUCID DREAM

In this dream I'd cleared the edge of a cliff –
carwheels spinning in air, half a mile up
in the afternoon. Death sparkled below
in an Alpine valley. Bluebacked snowpeaks
performed a symphony in mountain
above the spruce green spruce we'd crash in.

Life was over and for seconds I knew it.
I turned and looked at her. We'd neither
sit by a deathbed – which one first?
I kissed her. 'It's over!' I said. 'Our life!'
But then I was at the wheel, steering,
hang-gliding to the soft snowblossomed spruce.

Down we sailed and their branches yielded.
We munched silently into their soft receivings,
down through snow into earth, and so
to sleep again and haven't woken since.
Crises are like that. You're alive
for a while and then the lucid afternoon
fades as you munch through snow into sleep.

ASSISI AND BACK

It's the train from London to Assisi,
a sort of pilgrimage:
in the diner a dark girl
is staring: I feel my age.

It's the train back from Assisi, and the same
dark girl, suddenly aware.
So she smiles, sits close, intensely
close, and deplores her stare.

I'd like to say, You're lovely but,
as I'm old enough to be
your daddy, a man
must keep some dignity.

But on the platform at the end I give her,
unexpectedly, a kiss.
Her friends shriek, and she
wanders off in, apparently, bliss.

It's pleasant enough
to remember her now.
'I' seem young and naive –
she showing me how.

But why was I afraid of her?
Is it cowardice? And this
convergence? Surely not
a hint from St Francis –

knowing so much more now
than under his vow,
united properly with poor Clare
up there?

THE HISTORY OF LOVE

Olga Wadsworth went off to America when I was five.
              I never spoke to her, let alone touched,
                          but once
              I invited her to my party.
She was desked in sunlight on the other side of the classroom,
                          with golden hair and shafted eyes.
After she left I saw her in lots of American films.

Marjorie Green pulled her knickers down
              under a mac on the hillside above the Park.
                          When we came out of the mac
I could see Kenneth Marshall shooting for goal down below
              in a bright jersey, free from sin,
and as we looped past the goalposts he grinned as if he knew,
              and his white pants were filthied with muck.
Next Saturday I played too and slid as much as I could.

Mary Priestley was in the bathroom when my mother came in
              and we were all looking at each other's bottoms.
                          She was sent home with the rest
and my mother wouldn't speak to me all day.
                          There was a turd in the potty
              that Mary Priestley had left, and it looked
                          warm, dirty, black and guilty.
              I didn't see her for a long time.

Then I recited a poem at the Rechabites' Poetry Competition
              and won and was invited to join their Concert Party
as a compère. I wore a wig and a velvet suit like a lackey.

Mary Priestley was in the chorus,
  dancing with long legs and knickers,
  powdered and stamping and kicking in line.
   Those girls were never shy:
     they made me shy.

   Once in the winter streets
I found Mary Priestley playing at night
  and I played with her.
And later I was moved up a form and entered her class.
  She wrote and whispered 'Pass it on',
   and the note said 'I love you'.
    Hot, I wrote,
     and later in the playground
ran up to the gate between us like an aeroplane
and threw my letter over like a bomb:
     'I love you'.

Now I'm married to a girl called Mary who comes from
         America.

IN SPITE OF EVERYTHING

In spite of everything, I think
mainly of you, even though
this is the century of mass death,
gas, squandering of resources
and pollution of the future.

Though our grandchildren curse us, as they will,
limping and tottering with the diseases
we dumped on them through war research and industry
and millions are lying belly-bloated in Africa,
I think mostly of you.

Though trees are dying, I think
mostly of you, almost all the time, wondering
if your smile is an acid rain, or if
you really love me, and I can't have enough
of your unattainable presence and perfume.

Most of all I long to know
what you're thinking really, and this
obliterates the kneecaps blasted off in Ireland,
the profits from sophisticated weapons,
state terrorism, daggered idealism,

big dealers lobbying the government,
the investment of labour and wealth in futility,
the expense on defence on a planet
that's been indefensible ever since
the last of England were singing 'There'll always be an
England'.

REFRACTIONS

We can do no great things
but only small things
with great love
says a mother in Calcutta.

An old man kneels
round his wife's grave
hedge-clipping grass:
to serve, to grieve.

A dead seagull in a flooded ditch
on a dark night
has one wing raised
as if for flight.

An elaborate lamp
reflected in the window might
make it seem
as if there were no night.

II

'What is the answer?' No answer came. She laughed and
said, 'In that case, what is the question?'
  – Gertrude Stein's last words,
  recorded by Duncan Sutherland

GREECE 1950

1.
The Aegean's still a solution
of lapis lazuli:
brindled fish stare
and fin though filtering light like fish in tanks.

You plunge in – take a nostril-shock at how
epochs of tiny
lives flash and flow
in your blanched rush of flailing shanks.

Tasting thick salt, you know it with skin,
pump breathless,
headjerking, chin
up – eye-smacked by blue Peloponnesus flanks.

You and the terrain are new: a face or tomb
lit by stained glass –
made love to
by a girl whose mother's dying in the next room.

2.
Two people will
always be sitting
on the island of Spetsai.

Over their shoulders
Hydra turns purple
as the indigo sky
goes dark.

In his kitchen Stavros
is frying their
camel steaks.

If there's a way
to a forgotten life
we must have been seeking it
when we went so far away.

CHANGE OF ADDRESS

Some people have a lot of names:
Shirt, Shirtie, Bert, Bertie.
Lomas perturbs; but only
Herbert's embarrassing, deranges the who I am.

Names change at some cost like houses.
Each is an ambience; you squat in it,
display it, deploy it, housewarm it.
On parole, inhabit the language's character.

Who can abide the selves you find in the street –
the rich relations of someone who's
long been found missing – so
simple and incredulous and unwise

he hasn't found an idiolect in the language?
Every lover, every friend, every colleague
creates him. It's only at funerals
people find him, calling me Herbert.

The changes of address have gone.
My visiting card's the name my father called me.

ROUND AND ROUND

The Sun's the same Sun
in the Green Leaf and Blue Ocean.

The Sea's still in motion
though the rivers are flowing
and the vapours going.

The King knows who's King
and behaves like one.

The Child knows without remembering
who his mother is
and behaves like a Son.

MOTHER SKIN

That arctic fox my mother used to drape
around her bosom seemed to snuggle in
its tail, nipped with a clip beneath its chin.
She'd fluff it up and nestle it round her nape
and over her pearls and cleavage, scented shapes
like the brylcreamed bowler father brushed with firm
and cleansing swipes before she took his arm.
I loved my parents through these smells and drapes.

Furs and hats are soft and hard, furs speak
of mother skin – any fur will bring a reek
of powder, graze the cheek, though never actual.
Smelly monsters every infant breeds
make for a hundred hairy grown-up needs,
though furs have meat stripped out and bite their tails.

NIGHTFEARS

Clambering to dark on the top-floor corridor's
row of moonlit rooms, you meet those eyes
and bony legs stalking the draughty floor.
You snatch the switch, to exorcise
the creaking boards and the paper faces
that ogle through the wall their old grimaces.

You sleep in shirt and pants, too scared
to be exposed or dowse the light.
Why was it no one cared
to tuck you in or say goodnight –
or noticed creased-up pants, the smell?
Why were you too afraid to tell?

And what to dream of in the dark? At times
you're a crew, wrecked in the arctic sea,
slipping their dinghy, to die betimes,
not linger in mist: choosing to die,
you know that moments later a ship will find
the man who chose to freeze and stayed behind.

Why this fear of the dark, this reluctance to tell?
New islands shine, new fauna and flora
mature, emerge, ripen, swell
and rot. Still at the tiller, there's Horror,
but you, strapped to the mast,
tune to blue night, coming, and coming fast.

GROWING UP IN THE THIRTIES

1.
What day of the week was it – a Sunday?
He heard his father's shout upstairs and ran,
smelling the gas. She lay on a divan,
fishmouthed, unbeautiful, a face of whey.

She's still his mother, he loves her still.
And yet her face – it's like his grandma was
in the coffin, her sharpened nose and toes
when, forbidden to peek, he did for the thrill.

Or Antarctic Scott in the white film of those
losers in blizzards, drudging from the Pole:
cut off from affluence, the dressed-for-dinner role,
they pass their dead friend's grave and icicle nose.

Outside: flies heatstroked on the burning flags,
the boy next door bouncing a ball, trying
to dot them. Now he must hide his mother's dying.
As flies to wanton boys – school-Shakespeare rags.

2.
She can never pass a mirror. It feeds her greed
to know she's there, suddenly grey: a gaping beak
famished for herself. Yet Sybil, matriarch,
Rochester's wife: medium and mother in need.

Bony hands are clasping, can't stop wringing.
Legs must pace. Insufferable energy drives
the suffering machine: handwashing wives
can act the Lady Macbeth, neck tendons stringing.

Set books at school are all about his home:
Paradise Lost, the sulphurous lake,
Rochester's secret, the visions of Blake.
Quo Vadis makes the room a burning Rome.

Out on the Rec, the click of a cricket bat,
a shout, a cheer. On the swings Harry's
doing his Harry Roy. His crooning carries:
'This is yer old watcher-me-callum,' flat.

3.
Ruth stood among the alien corn,
loving to play her Haydn; also bright.
Not a great looker, or the sort to bite –
that the local lads'd feel and get the horn.

He loved her in his way, perhaps because
her life was not a matter of mere survival.
Himself, he summoned Beethoven, felt the arrival
whenever he beat C minor chords.

At the Gaumont he hardly dared to touch
her hand in the flickering black and white.
Her head's rigid as a sentry's, it doesn't seem right.
Oh! fear of rejection, oh need to clutch!

In the carriage back it's so difficult to chat.
Packed close with her's enough to make him hot.
Then down the train, a shout from a drunken sot.
It's Dad again, pissed, from a night out.

4.
Outside the house, the usual gang of cheerful louts –
one in particular known to have fucked a pig.

The grammar-school cap can make you look a prig.
'A chip off the old potato!' – the usual shout.

Dad knows they spoil the street and hates
the prick to his pride still more: he stalks out,
and they break into cackle, scuffling about.
The beast's on the street. It only waits.

Hard at his sums, he hears his dad brought in,
K.O.'d by the boar that's married to a sow.
Right's on that side, for Dad is snoring now,
death in his breathing, slaver on his chin.

The newsreels know the ghettoes: mugs like those
can smile and smile: now the fact of race
smashes a world of glass, or a mother's face.
So should one be a Charlie, thumb the nose?

SUFFOLK EVENINGS

1.
Evening's always a favourite time,
a lazy man's time, and autumn a favourite season,
for those who know they're living in failing light.
And failing light's internal. Sea and night
toil on but – it's more
of a vocation than a task. A ship snores
out of the scud, honking of risky work.
I turn to the fire and a different kind of dark.

An atmosphere close to pain; it implies
that all you've ever done, even your lies
and cruelties are invited: evening companions
to sit over tea or whisky and teach you sums,
equations once unteachable. Too
incalculable a calculus. On the pebbles, in a shampoo
of greening sea, bottle or dog comes back in surges,
always erasing us, of selves.

To the child who still hurts me it was hard to believe
in a time of no canals: so like rivers:
no barges now, but heavy with frogspawn and duckweed.
You dive off a lock into ink. From the balustraded
balcony at the back of the house, you could see
a water-rat launch in a widening and widening V.
The navvies are all dead, and what they left is a clear
stretch of almost stillness that's always been there.

2.
The tiny hands of rain on the window
rap a rainy Pennine childhood
in an eighteenth-century house

of pre-technological people: a grandma
born in the 1840s, an aunt
fifty already, my mother forty.
I crawl by the big black fireplace,
with the blackened copper kettle on the hob
that sings quietly by the flapping flame
as if we were wintered-in at Grasmere.
The huge kitchen's always dark:
lights burn by day; the only window's benighted
by the high bank glooming the yard at the back.

My dad's preparing himself a grog
in the stained-glass bar, I'm
on my farm with the lead sheep, drawing up
the drawbridge on my flagged fort,
or reading *The World's Great Books in Outline*:
pictures of Dante and Beatrice, my mother's
name, and *A Midsummer Night's Dream*:
Fuseli's vicious fairies: subfusc landscapes
with holes of light, no different from
the darkness under the table with the cat,
or the days of rain drenching the valleys,
or the watery window, where tiny hands are picking
and knocking and running down like tears.

3.
A ship snores out of the scud,
honking of risky work.
I turn to the fire
and a different kind of dark.

Evening: thoughts slip into night:
the flash of a lightship
just out of sight
has a name I've never found out.

A brass shoe dangles from my lamp –
bought just before that
cancer-test: a gipsy called,
and told me I'd live to be old.

On a sunny afternoon
the door crashes open,
a guitar string snaps; the cat sees
a nothing there – screams and flees.

A man on the beach,
with a gold umbrella,
taps it like a white stick: not only
deafened but blinded by the sea.

For another the sea's his mother:
she's telling him something serious
that makes no sense, as if
she were a piano, and he the audience.

4.
A white ferry strolls the horizon line:
a floating hotel, crystalline.
So much light and so much going.

Light as paper, seagulls
shriek and dip,
comparatively grey and dirty
with their angel-wings.
Sunset seeks the ship.

The other selves are creeping close tonight,
studying me: they made the choices
I didn't make. They lived promiscuously
with strangers for years and years,

becoming stranger to me,
with different wives and different lives,
taking the faces of strangers into their own.

A lightship
over the horizon,
invisible by day,
winks in evening wrack,
and, as I look,
signals knowingly back.

A ship snores out of the scud,
honking of risky work.

In the room there's an almost stillness
that's always been there
and tiny hands are picking at the window
and running down like tears.

SEA LADY

Someone's crept out of the sea,
lying on the pebbles, in pain:
a crippled labrador.
She raises one arm, a lady
in a siesta, languidly,
though night's falling, and this January rain.

Hearing my crunch on the shingle,
she's turning bitch-soft eyes and whiskers to vet me.
I'm coming too close,
and she growls, hisses and whispers,
tensing my tail with her speech,
though I know she can't get me.

Hurt? Perhaps she's tired?
But I'm too close, so she levers her spine
and flops down a shingle bank, enters the ocean,
periscopes twice with her head,
then hoists ashore,
crutching her legless rear up the steep incline.

Who'd be sick, if they lived in the ocean?
And who'd bark
so hard after fish, they'd give up the earth,
lose hands and legs,
freezing the warm blood back
to the cold, to feel after fish in the dark?

I sit in my lights by the fire, listening to Mozart,
reading Gibbon.
A Diocletian legionary, an old lag
looking for loot, found
a beautiful leather purse of priceless pearls.
He threw the swag away and kept the bag.

For what's no use can have no value.
And in the morning she
who loves the waters I left behind
is gone like a piece of flotsam,
a bag of pearls,
that is and always will be far out at sea.

THE WILD SWANS AT ALDEBURGH

Some days they look like outsize geese
with no secret, seen
waddling across reclaimed land
to a ditch. Thirteen:
my lucky number. But one, hatched out too late,
is without a mate.

The trees are in their winter grandeur.
A line of pine trees stands
aware of me as I of them –
children holding hands.
We watch a ditch ruffle like elephant skin
and the sun whiten and thin.

I track a curlew in a cloud
by its call: fast headway.
The thirteenth swan has taken off:
an immature grey,
it creaks a low flight, then stands and walks alone,
feeling its half-soul gone.

Pathetic these fallacies our lives fatten.
Forty years are lost
since I first read Yeats, yet I never see
a swan without his ghost.
A swan in death and I in life both read
the bobbin, rewinding the thread.

December sunshine brings white joy,
a milky hole in light.
These weeks three friends or almost-friends
have taken that silver flight
to some new pond or ditch or reclaimed land.
As souls, or swans, we stand

in a place of no giving in marriage.
Aware or unaware,
a leap through inarticulate light
defines some strangled prayer,
leaving us stripped, deciduous winter trees,
hand in hand, or on our knees.

IGNORANCE

I sit in the great ignorance,
in a vast church in a city of doors.
Workmen bang and boom: a restoration
beyond a bewilderment of floors.

In the nothingness where I sit
circling buses and taxies peal,
like the peel from an orange
that's eaten and once was real.

Empty space always amazes, the something
that nothing was, with wrapping moods.
And later, locked in, unnoticed, I thump
twin doors: they burst, and the lock protrudes –

a tongue, but whether for insult
or kiss, or whisper, it's difficult to say.
But tongues remind of love
and love is suffering today.

My friend is dead. The glass is broken.
Emptiness remains without its shell:
and emptiness speaks, and silence,
though neither speak well.

III

The word of the Lord came unto me again, saying, What mean ye, that ye use this proverb concerning the land of Israel, saying, The Fathers have eaten sour grapes, and the children's teeth are set on edge? As I live, saith the Lord God, ye shall not have occasion any more to use this proverb in Israel.
– Ezekiel *xviii 1–3*

from TODMORDEN

1. *The Vale of Todmorden*

This valley's beautiful not picturesque.
The folk who raised their heads to Stoodley Pike
had ears clubbed deaf by the ramming of looms.
The clog feet that clattered by the bedroom window
had squatted silently outside the peaceful mills
when humiliation threatened in the General Strike.
This is a cold country and a wet and the stones drizzle
on the moor sides and on the houses and on the tops.
The steep tilt of the valley drops the dark
fast in the evening: it's suddenly cold,
you're conscious of night. After the day's toil
toasted teacakes are buttered by the fire,
or water's hot in a tin bath with the flames on your skin.
The benighted streets are empty. The old houses
have black corners that seem occupied. Wind
buffets from Whirlaw to Stoodley, compelled by love
to the wisest and sometime cruellest thing
for the welfare of a people.

2. *The Black Swan*

Out of what black hole where my grandfather's standing
did I run as a boy? Behind whose parlour windows was I
                                        watching
the flies buzzing, tracing raindrop tracks, yearning?
Behind which bedroom window lay I in bed fearing
the damp-marks leering on the ceiling, hearing
the clogs of the millworkers in the morning,
imagining another track through buttercups, pollen and bees,
as I lay there with measles watched over by vampires?

It's a black swan that sailed past the black hole looking
towards my mother's and father's two windows
where they lay together suffering in their happier half-mad
days.

And later came the demolitions and the rebuildings,
the end of the stained glass, the creaking landings,
the ruin of the eighteenth-century irrationality,
the night-kept rooms in the right tangle for the family,
bats sitting around in a circle waiting.

The demolitions first and then the breakdowns
in a house that still exists though not in stone.

3. *Blood*

The shine on my grandfather's spectacles and his moustache
are what I remember of a taciturn man. He inhabited
a fireside chair in a household full of comedians
and jokers, an observer and smile, dipped in silence,
the dignity of the master-dyer. He trained only one
of his sons, my Uncle Jim, the eldest, in his trade,
calculating, of course, there wouldn't be room for more –
or ruled perhaps by the custom of primogeniture.
(My Uncle Jim told my father we were really Derby's.)
My father always lived with a sense of grievance:
he'd got to invent his life with the few resources
of one who left school at twelve and had no trade.
He brought out of my grandfather and my grandmother
a brilliant mind and sense of comedy, an observing eye
and a destructive melancholy, a reckless courage, a refusal
to bow, an indiscipline and contempt for forms. He believed
in truth and intended to practise it. I feared to tell a lie.
He was resourceful, too easily satisfied, and his mind
was never satisfied. He acknowledged the mystery

but refused it sense or love. He never budged
in his no to the injustice and disorder of the Verbum.
There was no God, and if there was he was no friend of his.
He was the troubled mind in a strong family, unbeatable
as a carthorse. For years and years my grandmother
kept her bed with arthritis till the end.
She loved a joke and flirted with her sons.
From that bed she behaved like a queen at her levee,
saying her no perhaps to the daily rising sun.
My father behaved like a prince disinherited and disguised as
a toad.

4. *Cornets and Trumpets*

In the first war my father was a stretcher-bearer –
in the Divisional Band. When the Battalion Bands
were broken up, they picked him out for the Division
above several bandmasters. Tested, he decided to play
his own improvisations on 'Rule Britannia'.
He got straight in. When the Battalion was stamping the
square
he liked to kick a football about where they could see.

When armistice came he was offered a Trumpet
in the Hallé Orchestra, but he turned it down.
'I'd a sweet tone,' he said, 'but I wanted
the musical background.' When I was fourteen
I longed for a Trumpet and got one through my Uncle Will.
We both used to play it – with the mute on –
till I slightly shifted a front tooth at rugby.

I'd learned to turn things down and once turned down
a fellowship. When my mother died my father
let the trumpet go with a pile of rubbish and my mother's
valuable clock: the lot for twenty pounds.

'You know, you could easily have mugged up anything
you needed to know about theory of music,' I said.
'Aye – course I could,' he said. 'I know that now.'

Brass band music on the radio's hard to bear:
all those euphonious, sad, sweet, masculine sounds.

5. Roomfield School

The school builders evidently thought of it as a Chapel
without a spire, Gothic but crouching.
It's a stone lid over the soil to culture this
horizontal plane where we go through the Market
and down the narrow lane by the Calder
to the Infants' Class and are distracted by the smells
of urinous trousers and individual bodies
and the hands raised to leave the room. On the sills
are the jam jars of sticky buds and the tadpoles
and at the break there's the sickly milk or the Horlicks.
We sprain our brains with arithmetic and spelling
and if we're good Mrs Graham will read us
The Wind in the Willows. When she goes out of the class
the little girls stand up and show us their knickers
and we write our reports on the books we've read:
'I liked it.'

                                                    This is a slot
where we're posted more or less carefully
and come out at the other end a different letter.
This is the stone school with the unmarried ladies
in their beards and long noses *in loco parentis*.

On the corrugations of the playground, where the rusty-
                                                    headed
policeman's son twice our size bumped
his chest against ours and twisted our arm, were we

really, like good poets, learning to erect
aspiring cathedrals out of our weakness? Why
do we need so much weight against us to construct
Charles Atlas muscles or tumble to
our weakness and give way? Why,
to slip through the slot of night, must we
be humped in a postbag all the day?

6. *The Rochdale Canal*

Hillsides fold down from breast-top to treed slopes,
the cut of the canal, and the banks we used to walk
to the baths at Shade. We bought pies or parkin
with the bus fare, dawdling by dusty waters,
munching the gingery bread and fishing for frogspawn.
We came out of history too, redundant by the railway,
minutiae of the landscape, like a Roman road or an abbey –
we're glands and ducts of Dame Kind who remembers,
to walk along, look in, to fish in, or swim.

The Duke of Bridgewater, an Alberich licking the wounds
of unmasterable love, broke off his engagement
to cast out coal from his park at Worsley, where
Brindley accouched what Bridgewater conceived.
Aristocracy, art and economics engineered
generations of big-muscled bargees whose legs, clogging
the walls of quiet tunnels of stone-and-water echoes,
backs on barges, gently moved their watery homes
towards a sparkling exit, decorated with children and roses.

Eighteenth-century couplets of arches sent water bridges
gravitationally over Irwell on great viaducts,
deep into the Duke's earth, cutting the cost in half
of coal in Manchester. Big money, navvies
and stonemasons spaded, chiselled and styled

still more of the structures of childhood, the weeds
of the Rochdale Canal, the aboriginal railways
with grandiose branching lines, mills natural as trees,
and minds transmogrifying the earth with money.

Diving off the lock at Springside I pulled myself down
through bitty water to the mud at the bottom
and watched waving weed and brown sunlight
till water power pumped me up again into sparkling air.
A dytiscid beetle trapped in those waters
wolfed a half-moon steak out of the side of my stickleback
in the night, engraving me with quick-rowing legs,
digestive tracts, salivary glands and huge triangular
mandibles for competitive feeding.

7. *Stoodley Pike*

The portico of Stoodley Pike's like the way in
to a tomb of gold-masked kings, but who's buried there
except perhaps the wind? The vertical orifice
of huge black stones was built by pterodactyls.
No light-slits brighten the stairwell. To be up
on the balcony you spiral a spine of dark.
The stone balustrade's built to hold you back,
audience to moors built for flying lizards,
your gob stopped by the strangling wind.
The builders were right. It's an inhuman height.
Ecstasy and nausea as your stomach dips
down the swerve of the opposite hillside reminds:
no one belongs here: you're not here for ever.
You're more void than the black stairwell
or the winds on the tops and the windier ways
you're going. The wind stops us speaking.

8. *Cross Stone Church*

When mothers die and they bury them
on snowy mountainsides in black and white
    Pennine mornings, after cold service
    in millstone grit unheated churches

sons will often bide at gravesides
feeling the ligaments of flesh –
    the other end of the cord
    now underground

tense as a worm pulled from the earth,
tugged and tugging back in a beak,
    taught the quiet roadway
    under the hill with the cars.

But sons, so tugged by ghosts and
guests, must move to the banquet,
    guests of honour, but guests,
    past flowers to the cars.

It never ends: on ventilated summer days
coasting the sun-patched moors in cars
    their mothers bought
    with money left,

driving the hills with well-loved wives,
they'll know they're taking the same roads
    down the intersecting valleys
    with the telegraph poles,

beneath Black Stone Hill
where they used to walk with their dogs.

9. *Fathers, Sons and Daughters*

In very old age at last, and longing for death,
my father, with just the evidence of the big body
and gritty will, remembered me roly-polying
and how fast I did it in Todmorden park –
and he made me choke at the two of us young,
he thirty, running faster than me.
Once he could hardly run fast enough
to stop me roly-polying into a lake.

Pear trees in the wind, blossoms
confettiing off in the spring, pears
bumping the ground in autumn: air in the tree,
wind oxygenating off the Pennines, or drenched
from the Atlantic, prevailing, knocking off
pears and people.

                    If science could do it
would you resuscitate every human being
who ever lived?

                              And somewhere
I'm always climbing down a cliff
with a girl on my shoulders. The sun's
a blinder, and neither will ever grow old.
Picnic in hand, a bottle in the other,
we climb down to the sand. But where's the sea?
That must be it – a glint over there.
And later, hours later, we find
the crack in the sea the sun goes into
and go back.

                    And somewhere I'm always
climbing the cliff with the girl on my shoulders.

The sands are behind. The hotel's gone.
The island's growing no older. The food's
for ever as good and always remembered,
the happiness, the wine, the big dinners, the talk.

10. *Millstone Grit*

Yes, there's the Pike, stiff black nipple
in the wind that strokes the sterile tops,
squeezing out stone for these cottages,
mills and churches, conducting blackness
into generations of sons that strut
the drystone walls with their teeth on edge.

Light can't nuzzle inside the cold cross
of Cross Stone Church but licks the four
black ears that tip the tower. The grit's
everywhere, in the cottage walls, in the bones
breaking out of the ruptured hillsides
with their crumble of afterbirth.
The hawthorns are prickly black,
the gravestones are black,
and as evening drops its cold
the moors go black, blackening the valleys.

Light breaks through the mourning, the clouds crack
and slant down light, the wind
jumps in your nostrils, makes your lungs rear,
and you know you've got it, whatever it is,
under your chest, behind your brain and mind.
The wind like lice in your hair is saying
what you only hear listening carefully and can't say.

11. *Buckley Wood*

A child's fingers trail and graze along a stone wall,
kissed and mollified by the scratch touch in the grit.
Beyond the wall the green-streaked beeches
are stretching their barks. The Viennese bandstand
and the mountain-soused green-upholstered park
have always been there. Steep up
and puffing you out, the Bluebell Wood
wades you on and on to bleed more white stalks
close to the bulb, squeaking as they break
stickily in the hand-wetting
drench of the long grass. A thick bunch
is bouncing and rainy, and their blanched stalks
glassed in a jar bring the long grass-root wetness
your hands went feeling inside the house.
The soaking beech trees clamber
their smooth roots deeper and out of sight
and grope with blind branches for a sky.
On a hot day a cloud of bees can set you running.
The sting of stone and bluebell skin and the blue
blur of bells put your feet on wet soil
and not in a haunted bedroom where the dark
is full of holes going out and out and on forever.

16. *The Town Hall*

The Town Hall's more of a Money Box
than a Greek Temple. The Corinthian columns
gesture to Greece but are no means of support.
It looks difficult to get in. The Elgin marbles
in the architrave allegorize the goodness, beauty
and home truth of cotton, wool and industry,
and the Fielden Monument, finger in waistcoat,
celebrates the Ten Hour Act of 1847 –

cutting the hours for the kiddies. Others
should have stood in the bays over the Entrance –
the pedestals are there – but no one came.

A crowd of straddle-legged and akimbo men
and no women are standing by the lamp-posts.
The pile they've built looks bigger
though not bossier than them.
They're straight-legged, straight-eyed, straight-hat
what-about-it hands-in-pockets kind of men.

19. *Dobroyd Castle*

To the infant me it had stood there for ever –
a megalith to climb to, uncontrived as the rocks,
natural as a Norman castle and unquestionable:
no more swanking or bullying than the stars.
Now it's the Fielden mind, battlemented, castellated
neat nineteenth-century stone masonry,
each stone like a brick. The homely oblong sash windows
have curved corners: it's a right-brain
organization of space. The men who imagined it
wore hats like mill-chimneys and rode light carriages.
Providing toil for the unemployed, hiring men to hew
a waymark of surveillance, now they're surveyable
as the castle they built. The more you look down
the more eyes stare. Your intangible fantasies
turn into mills and castles and a whole county.
The castle's like wearing a diamond the size of a boulder.

21. *Rochdale Road*

Horsedung and snow on the Rochdale Road
and the hens point their tails in the air

73

as they pick at the untrafficked,
unbatteried road. The streetlamps
are not much taller than the folk
and are modelled on giglamps or lanterns
on fluted columns. We used to swing
on the crossbar meant for ladders,
and my dad was once in love with
the lamplighter's daughter. White pots
sit on the trellis of the telegraph poles.
Tall pine-trees, wires and mind-forged
metal-contrived webs are communicating
a news the little boy doesn't know about
that will change his life. He walks
like someone going somewhere, not just
with two baskets to a shop. Is it
the feeling of coming from somewhere
that makes him lift that back leg
so briskly? And the other boy
trotting down those bulging
cracked-pastry causeway-flags –
they must have that walk from
plodding the snow moors that now
are cheek-cutting cold with their
starlings of dirt and white.
The houses are cosy. They've
comfy fires that have been cut out
of England by bare-waisted men
hacking and chopping long shifts.
The factory chimney's the pivot
of a Catherine wheel, but so far
cost-benefit's not dispersed
fancifulness from the lamp-posts.

23. *Haworth*

From Liverpool we could return to a strange country
for half-a-crown: three busrides, two changes
and we were up the steep Haworth street to a private winter:
invisible weekends in the Brontë Guest House
with *The New Statesman* in the breakfast room and
arctic sheets after nightwalks in the graveyard.

In the Black Bull bar we sat by the fire where
Branwell drank himself into opium.
We were all outside in our minds, hair flying,
Cathy and Heathcliff, windshouldering the tops
in the landscape of Emily's head,
with the gale in our throats and eyes.

This was where they watched each other
spit blood and imagine. Looking into her great
cat's eyes, I watched my astonished exit
into greater uncertainty. We watched each other
as lovers and our way of loving and into our loving
we dredged our own and these other lives.

IV

. . . pecca fortiter, sed fortius fide . . .
— Martin Luther

SOMETHING OUT OF NOTHING

He didn't tend to think of himself as an accident.
Yet, another evening, the telephone, a surprise –
a tadpole flick – and another sperm might win:
he might have been a girl with chocolate eyes.

At certain hours he dreamed he'd been invented
just as he was – or made himself: his turn
had come before the love began: the place
was right, he chose the lovers and rode the sperm.

He yearned at times for a timeless feel of self –
twisting back to his face in the silent Word
whose frequencies scored the gas and dust,
riddling logogriphs in the inert Absurd.

And he thought again of a photograph they printed:
abstracted majesty: a black man in the Chair.
Mechanics stooped around his loins like tailors,
each with the expert's concentrated stare,

putting last touches to electrical connections
in the art of death. And it was clear
the man had gone already from the chair,
listening to distance, far away from here,

knowing with surprise how he is loved, not where.

HELL

Hell was a place where people
dressed in the paraphernalia of totemistic
     pre-Christian cults,
horns, tails and hooves, grilled others
with the typical apparatus
       of medieval torture technology.

Hell, though instituted BC in the interests of
     Property and Caste,
seemed reasonable to the Christian
for frightening men of faith out of
       fornication, theft and masturbation.

In those days, if you went down to Hell,
you'd be unlikely to find God there personally
     supervising the torture,
or even Satan. What you'd find would be
       other Christians, under inquisitorial cowls.

And now, if you went there, you wouldn't even find
the medieval machinery, the thumbscrews. You'd find
     people in stiff white
clinical collars and no dangly ties,
explaining persuasively that Hell
       isn't a place, it's a State.

They'd be giving homely illustrations:
they'd be showing that Hell was the State
     of your choice:
that Hell wasn't Hell at all
in the old superstitious sense, but actually
       God's unbearable love for the damned.

If you went to Hell at any time
you'd find the full fashion range
      from dog collar
back to cowled Spanish Inquisitor
and forward again to cowled Ku Klux Klan
      or affluent apartheid

but never God. If you walked round Hell
at any time you'd find no trace of God:
      only Man. You'd find
that Man had landed on, conquered, colonized,
and impregnated with his peculiar smell
most of the places in eternity, from Heaven,
      down through Purgatory to Hell.

A VISITATION FROM BROTHER RICO

Brother Rico
brought his trombone
from Jamaica

and 'Man is God!'
said Brother Rico:

that was why he
never cut his hair.

And I wondered why,
wondered how.

WONDER WHY WONDER HOW
(sliding that bone)
AND THE BONE SAID GOD
MAN IS GOD
(Sliding that horn)
WONDER HOW WONDER WHY
NOT OMNIPOTENT
NOT OMNISCIENT
MAN IS GOD
WHOLLY MAN
UNHOLY GOD

A trained mind muttered
to the blameless face:
'If Man were God
no one would say it.
If Man were God
there'd be no word
for Man or God.
If Man were God

there'd be no Man
or there'd be no God.'

But Brother Rico
shone with HOppiness
omnipotent RicO
Don't make mOnnay
need an aigent
in this cOnntray, y'know . . .

WONDER WHY WONDER HOW
MAN IS GOD
(the bone said GOD
the horn said GOD)
TROMP TROMP
TROMP THAT BONE
MAN IS GOD MAN IS GOD

(the being of man is God?)

LAZARUS

Even then he didn't believe. He simply thought he'd been
asleep. We had to tell him he'd been dead. Naturally
we were all feeling out of this world, terrific. But gradually
well, his disbelief was too strong for us. You see,
it could all be a conjuring trick, couldn't it? Who could prove
he'd been dead? The heart can stop, the blood can stop,
and a man may not be dead. That's what the doctors say.
And we don't want to deceive ourselves, do we?

Pretty soon, of course, both of them were dead.
Catalepsy, you know, is fairly common:
people have often been buried alive. They're found
upright on the shelf of a tomb, constricted in a coffin,
or collapsed after hammering on a charnel door.
There *is* a sort of moral in this story, though.

JUDAS SPEAKS

Someone had to take a cool look at him.
Would-be martyr and messianic publicist,
he's got everything to make you love him
and everything to make you distrust him.

He stumps the country, lecturing to misfits,
undeniably curing hysterics, staging theatrical
so-called miraculous enactments of his message,
leading his starry-eyed followers
into a nebulous mysticism, and they're believing,
everyone's dropping into the delusion
that far-out truths are being revealed.

I love him, but someone's got to stop him,
someone's got to take a cool look.

He doesn't want to compete, spurns
the profit motive, despises what he considers
the rat-race, thinks we're being dehumanized
by a greedy society. He's no faith in
politics and politicians, says they're merely
promoters of self-interest groups,
distrusts all authority and social rules,
accuses the priests of being rotted by dogma,
legalism, literalism and state allegiance.
Well, maybe they are, but someone,
something's got to cohere. You can't
turn all values upside down at once.

                            He adores
spontaneity, but finds work tedious,
lives parasitically off the crumbs
of the Affluent Society. He wants a world

where everyone's happy and loving.
He styles himself the Son of God
and proclaims the reign of Love Alone.
These born-again fanatics offer
no formulated theory or blueprint
for the future. He merely urges you
to live for the day and swallow prayer
as the ultimate panacea. Insofar as
he's got any political aims, these are,
quite simply, to opt out of 'the world',
meant pejoratively. He's excessively permissive,
and his idea of redemption for the world
is to change consciousness through love and such,
and thus change everything. New heaven, new earth!

So far his followers are still a minority
among the quiet conforming majority
creating the Affluent Society,
but he does twitch a contemporary nerve.
His philosophy may be full of holes
but his followers aren't philosophers.
He doesn't know what he's stirring up.
Their bizarre ideas and behaviour
are gaining currency and his sayings are
slipping into the prevailing trendy jargon.
His followers don't work: they stand for
anarchy and nihilism. They're
good-hearted wrong-headed
non-productive self-indulgent layabouts.
His version of Utopia may be
naive and foolish but that doesn't
disillusion his horny-handed fans:
they lap it up of course, like the booze
he conjures up at his love feasts.
And the health-hazard's patent. He can produce
disastrous panics, toppling the neurotic

over the edge into madness, rendering
the unwary so helplessly confused
they physically do harm to themselves.
Deaths occur.

                    That being said,
it'd be unwise to underestimate
his long-term effects on Crime.
Toleration would be a disaster.
I've a responsibility to my conscience, my family,
and my loved ones. I don't deny
he fooled me too for a while,
and in a way it's my duty to atone.

                    Of course
some people will call this
a betrayal. But let them. I can't help that.

ST MARTIN-IN-THE-FIELDS

City churches aren't always easy
to pray in: there may be someone buffing up brasses
pianissimo, insistently, with cheesy
breath and a polish of rage behind their glasses,
sending almost tangible meditations
to distract our straggly congregations.

Or visitors delicately boggle at the faithful patients,
Guide Book in hand, not expecting religion
in architecture like this. Outside, the pigeons
drop little pats of white on assembled nations;
inside we pray, uneasily wondering:
whoever it is up there, is he listening?

Yet here bums in a blue-chinned Greek-looking worshipper,
pockets stuffed with evening newspapers, coat
flapping, and grabs his God by the throat:
he prays precipitately, wagging his head – a pew-gripper
pointing out to an old employer – what?
Is it horses? A tip flopped? A reproach or not?

And suddenly I'm in it: his grace has snatched
me out: over the altar the angels' faces
break the wood: they're reaching down with fact,
listening, embracing, swooping, and I'm hatched:
a broad white shell of completeness
has widened and cracked:
I'm open to sweetness.

WHAT SHE FINALLY SAID

Early August: acres of forest roast
in a cold moon, and two log cabins blanch
on neighbouring rocks. The ghost of love's our host

and night famishes on. We try to stanch
the flow of sex-hunger that makes our eyes
bark at each other, makes your arms branch

like shrinking laurel, and your shooting thighs
rise from the chair: anger burns with love,
feeding a blow-lamp in your eyes' surprise.

Their Botticelli blue will now disprove
they ever loved – too late, too late, too late –
because you did love; and yet the fierceness of

your face makes the cabin dissipate
into vacuum in vacuum, a bathysphere of space
in endless space, a bubble of no weight.

We see the earth's transparent face
as if a foetus witnessed from the womb
a grace beyond his little belly-base

as lighting sees through a set. A little room
is less than everywhere. And now you cry
'What is it?' and I watch your face assume

the look of someone looking at the sky.
Something splits and opens. You shake your hair.
I ask you if you think you're going to die.

We go to sleep abashed, ghosts everywhere,
patrolling the moonglow on the lake, inveighing:
'Stop hurting yourselves. Nothing anywhere

is what you think, least of all here, dismaying
though you make it. Love while you can.' At dawn
a knock on the door, a door-framed face is saying

what happened last night: 'Elsa is dead.' Drawn,
can it be, to the nearest friend, do ghosts bring news?
What she sowed at birth, she says, that seed of corn,

is now a head. 'The stalk lies out of use.
It's not the hell I feared, or heaven. It's far
more wonderful, acquitted unaccused!'

Our wake, as we row, is a low-roofed corridor
till our boat knocks on her rock and a smell of flowers
acid as vegetables. She's a corpse, and here we are.

There she lies, a girl now, slipped from the hours
and out of her moles and wrinkles, posting through
in packets of moonlight news of new life and ours.

Later we sit by her box in a boat that will do
to ferry her stalk, as we nose towards a warehouse
in a city that, in time, we all go to.

CLEAR NIGHT

August moonlight
filling the night
like a liquid.

Not a stir from the asp.

The alders begin to grow.

Galaxies, galaxies, galaxies.

On a night like this
dead people
can use the moonlight
like a telephone.

PRECAMBRIAN ROCK

I travelled a long way to Finland,
not really under my own volition.
It's a morose landscape that smiles in summer
and it's friendly to melancholy people, by not
being cheerful, only beautiful.
In winter the Victorian statues turn
abstract with snow, and it's as if
your past doesn't exist. In summer
the light flitters all night long
and changes every second and you realise
this selection of weather's the solution
of all the planet's history of climate
since the beginning, and so are you.
At times you're bigger than the stars,
and then you know you're
a member of the universe like that ant
and not responsible for yourself.
As you watch the high clouds changing
in the lake while you crouch there shaving,
you know you're just what you are,
and then it's gone, you're someone else.

BIRDS IN FINLAND

Mallards are clapping over the snow in an ochre sun.
If I go on looking I can imagine Estonia. Out there in Tallin
                                                    the soviet facts
must be seeming as real as these by now.
There are gaols on both sides of the Baltic.
All property is theft.

Who's the criminal is relative and depends on time,
like who is sick. Mallards freeze in
if they stick on the ice too long.
One's got to keep flying.
Look closely at a mallard,
and you see its got a neat white collar.

Nevertheless man's a social bird,
as well as a spirit. It's important
to know how dependent you are and still
keep some plumage. You'll never be an albatross
dipping to sloping seas and nipping up squid.
You're poised between pole and spin.

It's not much fun knowing this.
It's more fun to think you can escape
or be a bird. Are all these hundreds of people
you see in the streets, who never give it a thought,
part of the evolution of man? The answer is,
of course, yes.

MEETING

When I was supposed to meet you
to discuss my breakdown
the pub was full of drunken Orangemen
on their annual screw of the town.

I knew I was there on my own
but not why.
Had you put me there
to make me feel more alone?

My poems are all written to you,
even the scurrilous things:
especially the scurrilous ones –
trying to test your meanings.

You've sung to me in a pop song
and it's you who invented play.
If your cards are close to your chest,
I know you're not what they say.

Every day's a different story,
though I don't always see it as new.
I'm not always listening,
at least not always to you.

Who thinks they're way-out unconventional?
Let them listen to you.
You're utterly outrageous.
You've seen everything through.

You saw it before it happened.
In the pub you were really there.
You know I can never be without you.
You invented the notion of dare.

FIRE IN THE GARDEN

1.

> ... *per una selva oscura* ...
> Dante, *Inferno*, I.2

The room's so quiet it seems audible.
I'm here, in the sane words of a mad poet –
recalling my fear of madness that
made me ordinary. Perhaps madness
is our natural state if we get free.
I certainly spoke to God, in spite of badness,
and he, I thought, to me: grew up in three
short months – nearly getting me asylumed.
Still, as we know, no man's an island.
So then, just having a job, a toiler's fee,
a place to love, someone to help,
a disguise, to be more or less a self,
accepted as part of the crowd, seemed,
though never quite completely, the meaning
of being human. It's death, though,
we call madness and are afraid of, so –
we know our preoccupations have to go –
into a room so quiet it seems audible.

2.

> ... *si che ogni sucidume quindi stinghe* ...
> – Dante, *Purgatorio*, I.96

The garden stiffens as it listens to the fire.
The live branches hit staccato blaze
and the man crouches back and forth with his

deformed hand and pirate beard. The garden's space
is being cleaned, enhanced: do they know –
the slightly hunched trees – as they undergo
their pale winter survival at the purchase of so
much evergreen pain? The whole glade's
assuaged as the sun breaks. It deducts our gaze
from the man. We'd like to think about our roots,
but the cracking spits and snaps and the tongues
                                              unsmother
trying to get at the sun. The garden shrinks
at the man pitilessly making it beautiful.
Even in the sun there's that air of funeral
(though the fire's ecstatic) before the drinks
go round and the family rediscover each other.

3.

> . . . *la concreata e perpetua sete* . . .
> – Dante, *Paradiso*, II.19

Just to be still after the life of work
is a good death: the flavour of viaticum –
bouquet of wine in the rush-hour dark
towards fields of daffodils and clockless nights,
the stretching insight of elysium,
when the cigarette smoke in the committee room,
the bagpipe of one's own voice droning on,
the nuances gone and the thing ill-said,
the queuing years among red tail-lights,
the monoxide drive towards the amber loom
of whisky, the fall on the bed, the evening gone,
die, and the soul flies: a paper bird
in the garden, after the parrot is dead.

THE GREAT CHURCH HELSINKI

Every man who has faith in the Lord and lives in charity
to the neighbour is a church in particular, the church in
general being composed of similar individuals.
— Swedenborg

Grazing a purple shadow in the square
the body watches, timid and half-aware,
the mind's inventions – calling them a world.
The brain lights up, funiculi are curled:
aerial, elegant and immaculately risen,
a white bird on the wind, you pause
while the cathedral wakes and stares: a collision
of nerves becomes transparent as a bowl.
The structure of your molecules is the soul.
In every world a vision shapes the laws.

Brilliant in its cuts, a diamond mates
the silence of the jeweller and the stone.
Pushed boiling up through pipes of rock it waits
in darkness to be mined and priced and known.
Then bringing all its glyptic skill
imagination angles in and smites
a lump of molecules into a light.
The echoing brain we walk in overawes
with clammy dragon shadows, gargoyle jaws,
but galaxies burn when the mind goes on.

Still as a cloud of vapour in the radiant
intolerable ache of startling light,
intangible as heatwaves on its chosen gradient,
the Great Church shimmers, a weightless white.
Like all cathedrals, statues, cities – it too

seems to have stood here always, veiling, unveiling
the stealaway or vulva where the saints
absconded, though figured in bronze against the trailing
cloudscapes, gesturing to blinded flocks and their complaints
with green and vigorous fists against the blue.

Crossed by the purple shadows of your pillars
we sit on your sparkling steps and view the world.
An elegant Czar makes a long-since futile gesture
(with dignity, though, and whiskers rightly curled);
a ragged man is sleeping on the stone.
Meanwhile the shape of Jesus unobserved
waits on the lucid skyline, attentive, tall,
for the occasional startled face to pause and turn;
and round the corner with your place reserved
waits Peter's burly shadow, key and all.

DEAD RECKONING

And yet you've rusted in the belly of the whale . . .
Through sheer minginess timidly walked out
and exported your talent to sea. You bargained, for sale
where the work might pay and slipped down the gullet.

You thought – and thought again, starch in the whitening
acids of the mammal, delivered to its liver.
Hardly surprising, is it, if it's unenlightening,
fermenting in the must of money for ever and ever?

And then you're out and you let yourself down.
The inspirations change. And people scoff.
It's the prophet's lot: the huge gourd's grown,
and then the tinkering grub will kill it off.

Naturally you doubt those bursts of illumination.
The wind – it listeth: it's suspect even to clerics.
It's hair-raising too. Remember: hallucination.
The mind's a liar, delusive, prone to hysterics.

And yet she comes to you still, if you're ever quiet:
as filtered sunlight – specially for you;
soft through a window, picking you out,
for the new affair at the sudden rendezvous;

the café's warm at your smile: the proprietor notices;
the touch of her hand's a sauciness on your shoulder;
it opens your hope like a wallet: you're a sunlit lotus.
She's laughing at you. The sight of you older

makes her feel tender. Why had you got
so ready to suffer without her? Now you recall
her love that once was wisdom, in the not
quite normal quietness that unexpectedly falls.

PRODIGAL

At the last bit of the forest
the traveller nearly dies,
but he sees a cottage light burning
and it just keeps him alive.

So he gropes to the tiny doorway
and he drums like a man in a cell,
but the door's wide open even before
he cries 'Help me, I'm in Hell!'

And the Lord stands there with the turkey
and the Bollinger '94
and a carefully done-up Christmas tree
and angels there by the score.

But the man just bellows 'Help me!
Can't you help me! Save my life!'
So God reaches out with the turkey
and tries to give him a slice.

But the sot's still shouting 'Save me!'
So God leaves him there at the door –
leaving it on the jar though –
and warms His pants at the fire.

He knows there's no use talking.
He wouldn't know where to begin.
One day the duffer wakes from his sleep,
and when he does he's in.

V

Dr Weiss, at forty, knew that her life had been ruined by literature.
– Anita Brookner, *A Start in Life*

SOME NOTES ON THE LITERARY LIFE

1.
Loving a girl in every nook
that's the story of Herrick's book.

Chaste I lived, without a wife –
that's the story of Herrick's life.

2.
Jane was one of those happy authors
      who've no history or self.
She'd no adventures, didn't travel,
      saw little of London but much of bad health.

If Emily Prunty had coined *Wuthering Heights*
      would the book have caught?
The passion's consuming but isn't physical,
      and for Dr Leavis the book's a sport.

Emily wandered the moors with Heathcliff
      opened up to her God,
proved denial of her soul was death,
      and died of consumption at thirty-odd.

Jane kept the sitting-room with her pen:
      sensibility wouldn't do.
She proved denial of the code was folly
      and died an old maid at forty-two.

3.
Cavafy sloped
into Heaven
at a slight angle.

God heard
but said 'OK –
I've changed
my pneuma:
he can stay.'

There'd been some delay
about Judgement already –
so the scoffers would say.

'But a thousand years –
it's a day. I'm infinite.
Don't think when you think
I hadn't thought of it.

'In fine,' the Lord flashed,
'there's been so much
judgement passed, I want mine
to be the last.'

AUDEN AT HIS VILLA IN ISCHIA

The poet's still closeted with his talent,
even in the open air. Harassed, wry,
would-be relaxed, martini in hand, he'd
like to give it a holiday.

He won't be happy till its screaming stops,
and that won't happen till he's drunk and smoked
him and his talent to a good death.
His face is the map of its wigglings:

journeys of the soul on an old stone
it's his job to decipher. Meanwhile he keeps
reminding himself to keep on time,
run his accounts straight, and his talent lets him –

provided he gives it breakfast very early,
devotes a day to it. Even then it needs coddling:
the crosswords, the mysteries, the anagrams
that help the thing to overcome its tantrums.

The talent's perfectly fair: all it wants
is total attention. Get that, and it can be patient.
If it screws his muscles, never lets up,
it does offer bliss when he's been good to it:

an ecstasy – what ordinary mortals
ordinarily feel at weekends, out
fishing, or with nothing
particularly to worry about.

FAILURES

Donne deserved hanging
for not keeping
of accent.
Edward Thomas got a pranging
from friendly fire
the British sent.
Hopkins was snarked
by the exams he marked.
All nullified
at a tether.
It's not pride
but huddling together
that keeps you identified:
all considered failures,
put on the shelves,
not least by themselves.

'I AM WHAT I AM' – YHVH

'I am not what I am'
– Iago

Wordsworth observing himself
wandering lonely as a cloud

began dramatizing himself
wandering lonely as a cloud

and soon was describing himself
wandering lonely as a cloud

and then flashed cloudlike
on that inward eye that is the bliss

of solitude and then was dramatizing
that inward I . . . and then he was . . . revising . . .

Later all these I's go out
in the night and I watches them going

and we all go out in the night
and I watches us going.

EZRA POUND IN OLD AGE

Clouds are black and blue and white and grey-blue.
That wall of old brick has prancing shadows on it.
I've suffered history and tried to understand it
and failed. Let it explain itself then.

A child knows when it wants to cry, and an old husk
when it's finished, blown along in the light.
The candle flickers as daylight comes.
A child's right is to cry, but age's to be silent.

No one understands history. But there seem to be gods
and to walk by cypress and olives is perhaps enough
in age and in youth. Especially if the sea crashes
below on the rocks. There's a grace in being wrong.

Perhaps it's enough to leave the world with this knowledge.
Enough at any rate to make you seldom speak to outsiders.
Whose fault is it if I disconcert by staring them in the eye?
Or go to dinner parties and look into the distance?

VI

Remember the country and the age we live in. Remember that we are English, that we are Christians . . . Does our education prepare us for such atrocities? Do our laws connive at them? Could they be perpetrated without being known, in a country like this, where social and literary intercourse is on such a footing; where every man is surrounded by a neighbourhood of voluntary spies, and where roads and newspapers lay everything open?
– Jane Austen, *Northanger Abbey*

HAMLET

Every generation has a ghost: suddenly
history's here, stinking of corpse-flesh,
                    claiming
            your name and arm.

Your uncles were killers,
and it's your job
                    to set it
            right, O cursed spite, etcetera.

And every generation feels
the same. What we really want to do
            is write, find
            verbal solutions for the universe

or just hang about with our friends
making the grown-ups feel uncomfortable.
                    There's something
            rotten in the state all right,

but you *are* the state.
Easier to go abroad, wherever
                    they send you:
            England, Vietnam, or Aden.

You may get killed or kill. You go.
Or if not, there's sleep, suicide,
                    or the pleasure of
            dreaming. Hamlet.

He at least did do the right thing
with his last breath, though why then
            hand it all over
        to that idiot soldier Fortinbras?

Does every generation have to have
that ghost, and did he know it? Anyway,
            here we are
        in Denmark, still ogled by Claudius,

with a new Polonius, O cursed spite,
etcetera, and shall we do
            the deed
        before we die, and put it right?

RAZMAK

My most intimate relationship with a strange Indian
         was at the end of the war.
At nineteen a whole straddle of history
         had lugged me
to a fortress of barbed wire,
         walls and towers,
where red-cheeked men in pagris
         strode along,
each with his own rifle.

At once two Garhwali havildars
         were thumping,
kukris bouncing, like rabbits uphill,
         and me behind,
like their scut, weakening,
         while soft-nosed bullets
gobbed up stones round my toes.

Then I was a bird
hovering above my body, watching me running,
         ready to take off
if the silver cord were loosed,
         knowing someone
two thousand feet away in a turban
         was ogling me dancing
on the sight of an old and inaccurate rifle.

Fast reloading
and hoping to burgle me of my
         nineteen years,
he killed a mule, the bullet
         inching in
and cratering out.

My body reached the rock.
        Feathering down
and crouching with the havildars,
        I grinned,
we laughed, and mortars moped.

Was it really so strange
        that an unknown Indian
should take such a personal interest
        in an Englishman's future?

MURDER IN THE PUBLIC SECTOR

Hemingway had already killed
a hundred and twenty-two –
the sures besides the possibles –
but the last was worst:

'Let me take him' – with
a fast reach for an M1.
The blast gets the boy in the spine,
tours through and out the liver. The Hun's
about the age of Patrick, Papa's son.

Papa gives the kid his morphine –
nothing can be done –
and his bike to an orphan
whose own bike's been
nobbled by the Huns,
with 'Get the hell out of it –
back to the estaminet.'

The last man Papa killed
was actually himself. He rose
on Sunday before seven, pressed
both barrels of a Ross
to his brow, rested
the butt on the floor and drilled
out of the entire cranial vault.

In my dream Hemingway was skinned
on a sierra in the wind
with a white beard and a worried face.
Back and forth, back
and forth he passed
a cut-throat razor through his neck

unable to understand why
he was unable to die.

Winston Churchill planned
to finish six cities
and three million folks
with a dose of anthrax
and let Germany be
a sadder and a wiser land.

A romantic pragmatist
he'd no time to spend
on 'these psalm-singing defeatists'.
Anthrax is a form of cancer
that makes your skin like rubber.

Churchill took a time to die
even after he started.
Was he blocked at the Styx
by the crowds still going over

the Guinness-and-champagne
black-velvet waters
across the fosse

to the plains of light
where the only V-sign

is a crucifix?

ROSES ARE BLOOMING IN PICARDY

The Sudanese grips his enemy's balls,
shrills victory, spits on his opponent's prick
and slashes the scrotum, which, conscious, quick,
ejaculates in death, as a hanged man falls;
the victor's semen spurts on the softening genitals.
For warriors like these, a battlefield slick
with slime and bleeding men is like a picnic
of deflowered virgins for heterosexuals.

Owen wouldn't speak of the delight of war
to those at home who didn't pay with blood –
but knew the rabies of battle: the toreador
alone – and curse the impresario – should
taste the fine delight that fathers more
than normal taste for sex has understood.

A PRESENT IN THE PARK

Why try to keep guns out of sight of my son . . .
For God or the Devil or Chance came in
and crossed the park disguised as a man
and told the *au pair* he found this one –
a handsome curlicued six-shooting thing
with a Victorian cowboy's handle on
and a style of life and death for my son.

I've a dream of sometime going again
to the spot where the stranger came to my son,
and I'd carry a basket with candles in –
Lovercraft phalli for other men's sons.
Arrested, I'd show to the TV screen
the political point my gesture had been:
the tools of life are never obscene.

But I've started buying my little boy guns
to come to terms with other men's sons.
Let punching and killing be done in fun:
The 'growns' know how to hit and when.
Which peace my son'll fight for then,
and how, if at all, it's his to choose. But stens
of the mind'll be needed again.

The ocean's an endlessly altering school:
it flows in the wise and it flows in the fool.

THE PAPER GATES OF JERUSALEM

*For the earnest expectation of the creature waiteth for the
manifestation of the sons of God . . . Because the creature
itself shall be delivered from the bondage of corruption into
the glorious liberty of the children of God. For we know that
the whole creation groaneth and travaileth together in pain
until now. And not only they, but ourselves also, which have
the firstfruits of the Spirit, even we ourselves groan within
ourselves, waiting for the adoption, to wit, the redemption of
our body. For we are saved by hope: but hope that is seen is
not hope: for what a man seeth, why doth he yet hope for?*
– Romans, viii 19–23

1.
Plants are exuding effluvia
when I'm not there, and so am I.

But my cat groaneth together in travail,
hungering as for pipesmoke in his yellow pupil.

Especially that seed of soul he caught
from kneading his human mother is distraught.

Stroke him a while – he can't be satisfied:
hyperactive, prowling anxious-eyed.

Hunting's nervous: his little black head
came hunting out of his mother, hunting his need:

hunting in me, in my eyes. My eyes
hurt him, he blinks. His famined heart rises

everywhere, and everywhere's waiting for a self.
I'm waiting for myself myself.

Yet I'm stopped at that: Herrick would be surprised
at that roadside rabbit, with huge bumps for eyes.

In an age of civil war who can still
say goodbye to the daffodils?

If I'd a telescopic gun, someone said
I could manage to blow off the back of my head.

2.
The plants are exercised
            about a problem:
Rain: a right or a privilege?

In the back window a sign:
            Give Blood.
In the back seat a toy
            crab the colour of
            arterial blood
            dangles and bounces.
In the front seat the head
            turns: the eyebrows
            are pencilled black;
The canines are huge fangs.

When asked how he earned his living
            Dracula replied:
            I have private means.

He was painting a picture of Oxford Street.
Suddenly he realised he'd left himself out.

He started to put himself in the picture of Oxford Street
but then he became aware he was painting the picture.

He painted a picture of himself painting a picture of himself
painting Oxford Street and then he painted a

picture of himself painting a picture of himself
painting a picture of himself and suddenly disappeared.

At that moment Oxford Street disappeared.

3.
The Mullah Nasrudin was picking some flowers from a
hedgerow when he saw smoke. Some farmers were burning
wheat.

'Why are you burning that wheat?' he asked.

They smiled: 'It makes the money wheels go round,' they
said.

Then he saw some dairymaids. They were putting butter in
the cow-troughs.

'So why are you feeding those cows butter?' he asked.

They smiled: 'Le Général l'a commandé,' they said. 'Et nous
n'avons pas de gateau.'

Soon he came to a château. A baron was standing beside a
lake of, apparently, blood.

'What's that, then?' the Mullah asked.

'Wine,' the baron smiled. He looked towards the hills. 'Those

are the Meat Mountains in the distance.' He waved and
walked back to his château.

The Mullah was reduced to his component particles. When he
reconstructed himself, he was in the United States, where a
farmer was wetting his fingers and counting the dollars.

'Quite a lot of greenbacks there,' the Mullah said.

'For laying off land,' the farmer smiled.

The Mullah sat down by a river. He looked at his bread and
cheese and threw it in the stream. He opened his wallet, took
out a salad of greenbacks and began munching.

A little boy came up. 'Why are you eating all that paper?'

'Trust the economists,' the Mullah smiled.

IV
It was the Western end we found the gates at,
and they were entirely made of paper,
with heads of kings, queens, dollars and pounds on,
like playing cards, souvenirs or something.

So we sat down, talked, someone played with the latch,
and there was this fool playing with a match –
and someone tried to stop him, many did, too late.
Long wait. Then someone said, 'Well, let's go in?'

ECONOMICS IN ALDEBURGH

*Fundamentally, there are only two ways of co-ordinating the
economic activities of millions. One is central direction
involving the use of coercion – the technique of the army and
the modern totalitarian state. The other is voluntary
cooperation of individuals – the technique of the market place.*
— Milton Friedman

Living here, between a nuclear station
and the sea-wall tides are slowly battering down,
everything's privilege, peace, stagflation.
Easy to be content with this little town –
content! No sign in that of economic health:
one ought to be chasing utilities and wealth.

Economists know that man's a maximiser,
his aim to maximise both wealth and pleasure.
War's fun, utility, and makes us wiser.
To give's not human. Enough's no treasure.
Freed man has learned the way to be humane:
the market maketh man and makes him sane.

The myth of a mixed economy's evasion.
The market has no need of public pelf.
Coercion's inessential to civilisation.
The market's free: you're free to sell yourself,
be sold, or unemployed; it's funny
how people hate to work but do love money.

A maxi-miser: man's a mini-miser in this locale –
miser of his uneasy, guilty luck.
The only defence he needs is against the real:
a sea wall, death, failed life, his love unstuck:
no money for these, unlike the planes and tanks
he buys to fight the reds or please the banks.

ANYWAY, IT ISN'T SOMATIC

It's impossible to be a conformist
unless I stupefy myself with smoke.
             As soon as I give up smoking
             I get notions:

like, why not try some new ideas?
But liberty, of course, means
             a rather frightening
             polymorphous kind of freedom.

Byron, for example, why did he escape to Greece
instead of creating a society
             for the protection
             of good ideas?

And what about the long overdue Leisure Party?
Even with planned obsolescence, meat mountains,
             wine lakes, and
             subsidised idle acres,

can we make buying and selling money
the main business till the big bang
             reverses and contracts
             towards the crunch?

Must we admit we're snuffing production
to buck up the rationing system?
             Can we really go on generating money
             as our main product?

127

The fear rises that Bingo would be
more harmless than banking, insurance
          and the bourse, even though
          computer games are fun.

As the smoke clears from my cortex,
I start to visualise a new
          eighteenth-century aristocracy,
          for us all.

The cabinet appears on the media
and tells everyone that toil
          and money are
          poisoning output.

Their wish to conceal that superabundance
slashes prices and prosperity
          is bad for business
          has foundered.

Be satisfied with free cars, they say,
free food, free televisions, free
          washing machines and
          toiling automatons.

A simulation shows a man
feeding his old car into the recycler,
          selecting a new one
          and driving off.

He puts all his garbage
into an orifice under the sink
          where it goes
          straight to the infrastructure.

The post office closes down
and is replaced by fax.
               Illusion closes down
               and is replaced by facts.

We see a call-up of the eighteen-year-olds
for two years' toil. At twenty
               they walk free to face
               the terrors of self-realisation.

But how will we escape with no wars?
Will we feel safe with sport,
               art, opera, science,
               social work, or yoga?

Shall we have to organise controlled
football violence? Or can we too live
               as aristocrats lived,
               content with inherited handouts:

killing birds, breeding horses,
training dogs, playing polo,
               giving huge gourmet picnics,
               parties and balls? –

devoting days and nights
to love affairs? Of course,
               those who love power
               can govern the country.

But can *we* live without fake problems,
or seek escape up mountains,
               or race aeroplanes
               upside down?

We may be here for millennia!
Can we spend them growing
            the sidewhiskers
            of the nineteenth century?

I must fill the void with smoke,
or vested interests preventing the future
            will seem a family
            of delinquent primates –

and they're my fellow-men!
So I'm waiting for some scientist
            to prove that smoking
            isn't caused by cancer.

'AVARICE & USURY & PRECAUTION MUST BE OUR GODS FOR A LITTLE LONGER STILL'
– Lord Keynes in 1930

To get up on time for the factory
you needed an alarm clock.

It was dark: the alarm clock
needed luminous numbers.

The luminous numbers needed girls
to paint on radioactive paint.

To paint on the numbers the girls
needed a fine point to the brush.

To get the fine point on the brush
the girls needed to suck it.

They died of cancer of the mouth.

As they died they didn't think
of freedom or poetry or who owns time

or who owns the factory or why.
But when they died it was as if

they were experiencing death for the first time.

VII

This quiet Dust was Gentlemen and Ladies
And Lads and Girls –
Was laughter and ability and Sighing
And Frocks and Curls.
                                   – Emily Dickinson

THE CHAPEL PERILOUS

As the car eased up
the long avenue past
the ruined chapel and the nuns'
graveyard to the heat-reflecting
rectory in the bird-whistling
silence and the almost transparent lawn, I
was several witnesses of myself –
almost a crowd in the solitude.

The crowd's always there to meet me.
The lawn seeded for centuries
and inhabited, and the house
that watches with invisible people
ready with their ordeals
I'm always almost expecting: the great beach
glittering in the distance with its distant cream.

HAUNTING

It's winter again: the vampires are sleeping badly.
There's a moaning in the cellars and the walls:
they're getting thirsty: old ladies
are shuffling out,
remembering.

A man looked out of the frozen lake yesterday,
showed me his fangs
before disappearing, smiling
and nodding.

Bones have shifted in the vaults, cobwebs are torn.
There's too much walking around
among the dead, and there are rumours
that when I'm gone
I shall be no exception.

Old bones in the bonehouse
will stir again.
Tall white ghosts will walk the earth
remembering.

ELEGY FOR ROBIN LEE

1.

People get very upset
when you take your life. You queue for it,
a warm takeaway Chinese meal, and sit,
plate on knee, munching quietly,
with music on, so as not to be sick.

Then at the tap, a glass to gulp down
the pain-killing pills, and, ready,
settling down in bed, with a bottle of whisky –
and an urbane, soothing voice,
continuing civilization on Radio Three.

The ritual includes a note,
absolving and thanking your friends,
suddenly scribbling faster
as the sleepiness hits you, knowing at last
you can't last –

this mistaken day is darkening out, though even now perhaps
though you're napping something's still ripening –
too late to wave now
as you look at an angel in Hebrew brightening
at the end of the tunnel of light.

Who'll say you were right?
Who even knows what we know?
Death's a two-way contract.
Some want that angel hard enough indeed
and have to try and try and try again, in fact,
and will not succeed.

2.
They find you in your bed,
in the dried vomit, the dead
whisky bottle on the bedspread,
the Third Programme
starting at seven *ad nauseam*

You'll not in this stiff mood
cling or sing,
no more poisoning,
with eight warming whiskies and eighty-odd
white tranquillizers in your blood.

You've given the last word
to a man who never met you: 'balance disturbed'.
It's instead of those words
that might have come through
in the dim academic days ahead of you.

Your life was hard.
If so, you've annulled it.
If the sun was too bright,
you've dulled it.
The pale face in the flushed sun
is ashes now in a darker one.

from ELEGY FOR JOHN RIDGEWELL

1.
He'd got nothing
and ten years he studied architecture
and bought and rebuilt a boat
and rented and altered a flat

and worked and paid his own way through college
and started a new love affair
and rented and altered a flat
and there was still nothing

a boat for someone else
a flat unfinished
an architecture unbuilt
a girl ummarried

some drawings
friends grieving

the moon phasing
the sun coming up
the river opening
strangers coming

and he borrowed a boat he never came back in.

2.
In his beard and black jacket
cold and a little hunched
with his six-foot-seven stoop
like a secular friar

cold and a little hunched
waiting for his death
like a longboned friar
after long penance

he would enter the sea
as if he knew
though we didn't know
she was already his

I remember him admiring her
round-eyed with love
though we didn't know he was going
feeling affinity of water

and though I didn't know
I looked at him carefully
seeing his affinity
and its quelling happiness

seeing his quiet ecstasy
at the sea that's always there
with its swell and quell
here, round us, in us

feeling it always there
feeling and being water
here, round us, in us
being and feeling water

though he's gone now, relaxing
in the shovings of the Humber
in the tidal unmasking
in the heavy Humber

the face that's gone now
smashed in the river's muscles
unwinding his eyes
in the river's currents

taking his eyes
from the drenched body
unwinding the face from the darkness
that's always conscious

before we're drenched
and before we're dried
in a six-foot-seven stoop
and a beard and black jacket.

WITH THE PIKE BEHIND HER

The end of the expedition:
brown eyes, like a fox's, keep
unbeatable lookout, not quite
human, retreated under light,
hearing perfect, though I thought she was asleep.

A hand crabs out from the bedclothes,
and I hold it: slightly moist meat, a crone's
fingers, blotched red, a forehead grown
like Shakespeare's, greying at the roots, knobs
protruding from her collar bones.

I sit quietly and pray: what comes
is her spry person, in her kitchen, frying,
smiling in the mountain house above Shaw Wood,
with Stoodley Pike behind her through the glooms,
making me feel needed without trying.

She knows I'm here – she asks about my children –
and who's looking after me tonight?
And: 'Don't you know anything then?'
So I tell her what I know – a mite
to the tortured body: all that's trite.

How my children often nag each other raw,
an ill-matched affectionate couple, both mules,
and flibbertigibbets; that my mother-in-law's
married again at nearly seventy – a nice deal;
and what we think of their schools.

Time ends, and I bend to kiss
her damp forehead and, leaving, acquiesce
in death, blowing kisses to brown eyes.

She says, 'I've been listening to a lovely story'–
blowing kisses back, more like a mistress.

And all the time we're talking, outside a window
some children and a dog or two
are laughing, barking, with a bouncing ball
in a sunny park, in a bubble of light, all
hanging like a bathysphere in the dark blue.

NUNHEAD CEMETERY

Unfindable as an elephant's graveyard: an address
always difficult to recall: wild undone
acres of estate in the sump of South-east London.
Too jowl-by-cheekbone for more arrivals, it's a mess
for vampires at night, but on brambly sunny days
a buzzing plot of elegiac haze.

Some find the blackberries stewing here delicious:
heat from gravestones and corpsemeat nitrogen
fatten up great black clots from juices of citizens.
Tasting one day, I was stopped by an inauspicious
glimpse: old thighs and shins spread out like toys,
turfed out by dogs, or necromancers, or boys.

No doubt cold-eyed killers have been
laid out here as well. I shouldn't specially want
the fruit of a gangster's guts; and those who haunt,
slow to let go of soil, are often mean.
Miming Oscar or Joyce, to impress, the ghost fakes
gnosis at séances and wakes.

The chapel's horny and spiky; a spirited evil's
crept into the crockets, and there's a smatch of more
than malice in its Gothic crouch: a sore
sourness of damnation, unhouseled upheaval.
Those who think murder a sport (a recherché thrill)
might find a campus here for a quiet kill.

Idiot, I planned to work here: a bright weekday
afternoon – a quiet spot, I schemed,
for reverie and writing; but soon it seemed
there was someone watching, or tracking my way.
Easy to cudgel you here – ripe place for a shambles –
and quick, in someone's grave, under the brambles.

Was there someone following me all about?
Yes: you'd think your companion in this retreat
wouldn't be quite so careful never to meet!
I left, but when do we ever meet? Peering out
at some we've loved since the playground and sometimes fled,
whom do we really know, living or dead?

HERON

The crematorium sits quietly by a river,
bosky, bird-haunted, willow-fringed.
At this double rendezvous,
fishing is dawdling by water
with apparently something to do.

Success is cruel: a fish flaps,
aghast at the thing in its mouth,
the net round its scales, the pain of air.
Yet a sharp smack on the back of the neck,
and the pain's not there.

The heron angles with no licence,
but glimpse a watcher, and he's off:
an awkward contraption with a glued head,
long S of neck, and a dangle of legs:
or a child playing airplane, arms spread.

In water he strides circumspectly,
not to tread on something sharp,
his knee at 90 degrees.
Feels down softly in the mud,
with his claws and his elbow-knees.

Apparently asleep or thinking,
he listens for fish. Long beak
pokes, gobbles, and his swallow
is quick. Stowed, he stands and meditates
and his flap away is slow.

Now in another place he works alone
somewhere beyond all this,
while the other watchers only wait,
scanning us from a new angle,
silently interested in our fate.

A herd of snipe are grazing:
hungry Chinamen
prodding chopsticks in a stew:
I'm absent; but once a lapwing
looked in my binoculars as if he knew.

THE BRIDGES THAT MATTER

The bridges that matter to me aren't the silky gleams
engineered over leagues, the glassy slivers
of light, or nervous ligaments of mist, deftly
flexing over rivers,

but the thundering viaduct of blackened millstone grit,
always dripping above the slaughter-house, and the chippie,
and through it the seedier streets, the boys' club, the park,
the prospect of Burnley and the Hippy.

A bridge is nothing felicitous – no mathematical six-lane
flow –
but a louring and whistling, rushed at by trains, a soar and a
rise
you undergo to a possibly promised land. I remember
the doggy tenderness in a calf's eyes

as a knife went into its throat: trust and dread
and a sad glazing before the head was spoilt with red.

SAD COWS

Horses have a sense of humour, but these cows
do not. Their slow gait has the float of hopelessness.
One hoists from the field like an old-age pensioner
who's called again to the loo and plods slow-motion,
humping, as if into a gas chamber, leaning
on her shoulder-bones towards a place that's lost a meaning.

It's as if they were in mourning for the sorrows
of all cattle, enduring in the *anima gregis*
their ancient failure of a purpose of their own,
their beautiful-eyed uncomprehending indecipherable
dossier of offspring slaughtered for some mysterious table.

WAY OF LIFE

Is it the ghost of Miles Weatheril, the infamous Vicarage
murderer, that stalks the corridors of the Black Swan Hotel?
– The Todmorden News and Advertiser

These rainy winter evenings make me race
back to the first steel of rain on skin
even in Greenwich Park, with economic sin
pocking the city below. Drenching the brick, slewed
along iron railings, down, across the road,
and up to Chesterfield's house, it cuts and cools:
something interested in your face.

The paths wind like life now, pluvious
corners but with mostly the expected there: no
dare except perhaps a mugging – a quick blow
like ice in the spine at a quick step –
that's only the darkling jogger. No: except
the gate may be shut, there's no threat;
and a shut gate's more like a hope, a plus.

A dog strains at its crap
and peers back vulnerably but trustingly
over its shoulder as I exit the gate. I'll be
fifty-eight today, a figure suggesting
eighty-five: a not-so-distant interesting
old geezer still fermenting, brewed in
the demijohns I designed from the original chap.

February seventh – the month my mother and I
chose for our birth, and the month my mother
died in as she predicted. Still, it's rather
kinder than many others. The English winter's
certainly the weather for reverie – hinter
at insight among the skeletal trees. With no
cold or rain who'd ever think or cry?

The house we live in is,
the rag says, haunted. Footsteps shin
upstairs or plod along when no one's in.
Glasses explode. One Sunday lunch
a whole tray of twenty went smash at once.
Beermugs slide along to the end of the bar
when there's nobody near, suddenly go whizz,

or keel and tip their contents on the floor
like men. Cellar barrels have their taps turned off
by invisible fingers. In the empty loft – a cough.
Heavily sprung fire doors open and shut
though immovably draught-proof and expertly cut.
A cur sniffs and stares, hair on its neck
hackling at a quiet ceiling or empty door.

It leaves me wondering: is it myself bewildering
the house, or mother, or father, deep in the quiz
of endings – back where it ended: happiness, that is.
New places made new faces: we went mad,
each in our pertinent ways. How much time, dad,
it's taken – to shed the spooks that tracked that house,
molesting my childhood and still maybe my children's.

VIII

Experience is the name everyone gives to his mistakes.
— Oscar Wilde

TWO POEMS ABOUT ART

1.
In the National Gallery

I'm sitting in the National Gallery cafeteria
where the tinned salmon sandwiches are a trifle expensive
and the intelligent well-brought-up
somewhat artistic girls come.

Particles of sexuality are
troubling the ether like lightwaves, or packets of energy,
and it's very hot.

The quanta come off in clouds from between their legs
and gather round male trousers, insinuating themselves.

Later I might go up and look at the pictures.

2.
Hot Day in the National Gallery

after Sassoon

Everyone suddenly started taking their clothes off,
the ladies in hats and the girls in leather,
and one girl started scratching herself,
and when people started feeling each other
in front of the Rubens and Piero di Cosimos
the attendants were mute.

Nobody told the police, because of the spontaneity, the day
everyone impulsively fell in love in the National Gallery
and did everything artists had only dreamed about

as if they were all in celestial bodies on the Astral Plane
or bacchanaling around in the Elysian Fields,

with the sun shafting in through the dome,
catching water, making wine.

VENUS'S FLYTRAPS

Victoria couldn't abide
a vegetable insecticide.
It certainly wouldn't be right
to encourage a plant with an appetite.

Victoria's daughter, christened Hope,
dreamed of Venus's Flytraps and Scope.
She had visions of them growing,
especially when they set her to sewing.

Felicity followed, an optimist,
who put them on her shopping list.
She planted them, to her husband's surprise,
and fed them daily with slaughtered flies.

The plants soon learned to need their
benefactress and feeder.
They gave her fingers affectionate nips,
and some days they kissed her on the lips.

SOMETHING, NOTHING AND EVERYTHING

There was nothing between us
then something took off her dress
something took off my shirt
something took off her brassière
and something took off my trousers
then something took off her knickers
something took off my pants
there was nothing between us
we touched each other
everything was touching between us
we kissed each other
there was something between us
then everything entered her body
there was everything between us
there was nothing between us

CHIMPANZEES ARE BLAMELESS CREATURES

They spend most of their time eating
or looking for food: i.e. working.

Or if they aren't messing about in trees
or absent-mindedly
pushing off their children
they groom each other
with great concentration
eating the salt: i.e. loving.

They're a bit promiscuous.
They share mates comfortably
without getting angry
and if a row breaks out
it's for no apparent reason
and suddenly stops
without anyone being hurt.

They cuddle and touch each other
a lot and there's much
curiosity in their sex.

Sometimes a mother will want to
join another group:
there's a fair amount of shifting around.
She feels very shy about it
and the new males
look her over
without tension.

Then she kisses someone's hand
and someone shakes hers.
She goes round

shaking and kissing hands
and she's part of the group.
No one makes much fuss.

Chimpanzees are blameless creatures,
and it's only if they're frightened
they'll tear your cheek off.

A CHILD OF THE SUN

When they crucified him to the lawn
with the croquet hoops, it wasn't because
he'd been staying up late studying Greek,
to see himself shine at the early morning seminar.

When he was hoping for a grant
he didn't even know dole queues
were stretching out impatiently, waiting for
champagne, with the rock bands blaring, and débutantes
enviously eyeing each other's flawless creations
and clinging to young men clawing uncomfortably
at white ties, murmuring their feet were killing them.

No one said, 'You're here to enjoy yourself
and be brilliant.' He'd never met
a Master of Balliol or an Arctic Explorer.
No one he knew ran an Export Company
or had a million-pound-a-year interest in
Keep Britain in Europe.

He didn't really blame this
on the social system. He somehow thought
it was because he'd somehow made some huge
prenatal cosmic mistake.

THE NEWS

Two men were shot in Sloane Square
this morning
when a masked robber
held up a bank.
One died, the newsmen think.

Miss Jayne Mansfield, the star,
died today
when her car
collided with the beyond.
Miss Mansfield was a blonde.

And Primo Carnera also died
this morning,
it has been verified.
He was said to be
the biggest prizefighter in history.

The Rolling Stones denied
this morning
that they'd lied
about the burning incense.
It wasn't to make the hemp-smell less intense.

The Rolling Stones also avowed
this morning
that the girl hadn't allowed
the rug to slip purposely.
She'd just had a bath and was waiting to dry.

And the first British reinforcements
this morning
arrived at encampments
in Aden by jet.
None of them are dead yet.

THE PAPERS ARE NOT AN INSTRUMENT
OF THE RULING CLASS

Lord Northcliffe was the only man
who understood the Education Act
        and benefited from it.
    He saw the significance of reading.

He said, 'If a dog bites a man,
it's not news; but if a man
        bites a dog,
    it's news.' Similarly if a country has

30 million abortions a year,
that's not news; but if foetuses started
        killing their mothers,
    that'd be news. In Paris

there are thousands of restaurants
that are not news; but there's a restaurant
        where you can eat people;
    that's news. They're freshly murdered

and you order in advance the parts you want:
breast, shin, giblets, brains, etcetera.
        The thumb's supposed to be
    especially good, and the coccyx.

A customer was convinced by a colour supplement
that war was fun too. He joined up
        and they burnt him to a crackling.
    They found his prick erect, which wasn't news.

RETREAT TO THE SHEETS

My cat approves of these long slow afternoons –
a day in bed, a headache, grey outside.
These days in bed are always opportune.

Despair's close by – and who can be immune?
You need new time – to brew unoccupied,
which makes my cat enjoy these afternoons.

Unless I can dream, I'm reckoned in a room,
but illness opens out new vestibules inside:
these dreaming days in bed are opportune.

Last night the sky was flaming with red festoons –
which happens when a wire and rain collide.
My cat prefers these long slow afternoons.

A counterpane becomes a felt lagoon
as I listen to the silk pacific tides
whose shushing makes these days so opportune.

You hit hot sand – and leisure to commune:
you're sick and draw the time your work denies.
And cats approve of these long slow afternoons.

Proximity – it brings these little healing swoons
as telepathically your muscles all subside.
Your eyelids droop on days so opportune.

Frail wings will only grow in still cocoons.
It all ends here. Why am I seldom satisfied –
like him – with these long drifting afternoons?
Such days in bed are, oh, so opportune.

GREENWICH PARK

Spring's come, a little late, in the park:
a tree-rat smokes flat S's over the lawn.
A mallard has somehow forgotten something
it can't quite remember. Daffodils yawn,
prick their ears, push their muzzles out
for a kiss. Pansies spoof pensive
Priapus faces: Socrates or Verlaine.
A cock-pigeon is sexually harassing
a hen: pecking and poking and padding
behind her impertinently, bowing and mowing.
But when he's suddenly absent-minded –
can't keep even sex in his head –
she trembles, stops her gadding, doubts
and grazes his way. He remembers and pouts.

IX

My endeavours tend only to unite and place in a clearer light that truth which was before shared between the vulgar and the philosophers: the former being of the opinion that those things they immediately perceive are the real things; *and the latter that* the things immediately perceived are ideas which only exist in the mind.
– George Berkeley, *Three Dialogues between Hylas and Philonous*

TWO OLD LADIES, A SCIENTIST
AND DEADLY NIGHTSHADE

Some years ago our most eminent botanist
found two old ladies
uprooting deadly nightshade in a lane.

Beyond the grey trees a sour moon
watched itself wickedly in the silver ditch.

'It's dangerous, you see,' they said.
A queer wind walked down the lane
and some bird chuckled in the bushes.

Our most eminent botanist said, 'Maybe.
But it's a rare plant
and besides England is overpopulated.'

And all day long the frantic ants
had hustled their eggs across a yard of earth.

SOUGHT

He came into the file as an intellectual enquirer:
he assumed that what high calibre brains had discovered
before would be found in physics.

He was no judge: the point was to be objective –
to leave himself outside, untouched, observing.
He could be a tape or perhaps a microscope.

Beginning in this disinterested, detached and critical way,
divested of all preconceptions, or assumptions, he was
disturbed to find he was somehow still there.

Not only was he not entirely outside his work,
his work was somehow looking back at him. He was
unexpectedly the observed as well as the observer.

One day, radiated by billions of elementary particles
as usual, he began to get a particular awareness
of being a subtle person in the bombardment of light.

YOU SEE WHAT I MEAN

And after all time may not be a dimension.
Could be it's only a miscalculation
                of a physicist who was, anyway,
                not very good at mathematics.

Not for a minute would I say we
in our unrealistic unwillingness
                to swallow the bitter pills
                had really been right all the time –

as though life were a fairy story where
the wise men were wicked magicians,
                who could somehow
                hypnotize us

into only believing our eyes –
falling back on the most invisible things
                to do so. Oh no
                I'm not so naive,

only . . . after all, Newton was wrong,
and think of all the poor sods
                who went to their no doubt
                uncomfortable graves

bravely believing the Royal Society had
somehow proved something they didn't
                want to believe. And now . . .
                supposing Einstein's wrong?

After all time may not be a dimension.
Perhaps it's only the equation
        makes it look that way.
          I measure the room with bottles, say,

and it's thirteen bottles long. So I add:
Looked at from another point of view
        the thirteen bottles
        are a room long:

the two items are reducible to the same law.
Therefore it's truer to speak of
        bottles-room
        or room-bottles

than make any artificial conceptual distinctions.
Not for a moment would I say this was true,
        of course, but
        you see what I mean:

people are dying without knowing whether $e=mc^2$ or not.

EVERYTHING

The whole planet's made out of lightning.
Put terminals to it and it'd flash
loudly at you. As you walk about on the soil
you can easily forget the oven underneath
and the oven underneath the oven.
Everything's cracking around like a whip
inside an egg just going to hatch out tigers.

But still, outside and inside all this
there's something cooler and more insulating
than cotton wool or lambs. If the world's
an incubator it was made by
cloudy hands. You can only assess
the cloudiness by listening to the thunder:
an absence that's as quiet as ultimate noise.

PRIVATE AND CONFIDENTIAL

There's not much point in looking at the stars: we know what
                                                          they are,
except that we don't know what anything is. Not to
                                                    understand stars
I rubbed them all out and then tried to invent them.
I made every star like every other star, except they were
                                                          different
like fingerprints or trees. Probably I didn't know
what the universe was going to do with itself.

If you go on looking at galaxies long enough they
and you go out and when you're invisible
darkness goes groping after darkness even though
everything seems to be disappearing behind points of light.

WELL, SO THAT IS THAT

1.
Christmas is gone. So it's time
to pick the tree of its stars,
pull down the candlesticks,
drop the planets, conceal the fairies
in the bone box with seven ways in.

But now it's Christmas again:
the stars glow out of the bone,
the candles flow like a Lady Chapel,
the fairies flip into flowers
and flap out like petals.

I can stop smelling my brain.
My nose is all the perfumes.

2.
The moon's phasing behind my eyes,
as if it were the slow movement of this music,
my ears are the sea, knocking at my
swishing generators of imagery.

All that blue space inside me
is punctuated with stars, my body
pricked out with primroses and bluebells.
I've dug into myself with coal mines,

covered myself with eczema and tractors,
swung over myself with cranes,
swilled myself with oceans
and dried myself with deserts.

I'm camels and whales I'm exterminating,
ship-selves cleaving through sea-selves,
and when I'm dismantled some day, will I
perhaps believe at last and be I am?

3.
Sometimes, watching each other,
no one that speaks is there.

Sometimes, watching each other,
we're only intruders who dare to be there

while two black angels
ogle each other with our eyes.

And sometimes, watching each other,
there's someone I'd rather not see,

not know about, watching me quietly,
seeming to need me

for purposes she doesn't know
and someone else will inherit.

4.
And in the morning we'll awake again.
I'll be with you, waking beside me,
and know your hair on the pillow.

Daybreak'll dawn in us
after the strange lovers of sleeping,
and I'll make you again.

I'll make you as I remember
who you are, and you'll make me.
We'll take up the tale where we left it off.

We'll swim again in the green lake,
catch the perch and the pike-perch
once more, and smell the forest and the flesh.

We'll feel the lake on our skin
and leave each other for a while
and go to sleep, and in the morning . . .

5.
The point thinks 'I can't go on'
as it edges on and becomes a line.

The line thinks 'I can't go on'
as it edges on and becomes a plane.

The plane thinks 'I can't go on'
as it edges on and becomes a cube.

The cube thinks 'I can't go on'
as it edges on and dies in eternity.

X

*Ma tu, perchè ritorni a tanta noia? perchè non sali il
dilettoso monte ch'è principio e cagion di tutta gioia?*
— Inferno, i. 76–8

LETTERS IN THE DARK

At Southwark Cathedral

1.

I lay awake writing letters to you
in the dark – so I got up, felt alone,
and put on the light. I need someone.
There's a kind of intimacy that's closer than the bone
and can sometimes get into letters, more than anywhere.
It's communion with the dead, or more like prayer.
The dead are somehow refined, or are being refined.
When they answer back it's in disembodied voices
from which all static and chatter stored in the cells
have been magnetized off, buried, or even burned.
In the purgatory of the small hours the person
God might have first imagined stirs on the rock,
pushes the vulture from his liver and begins to turn
his anguish into intimate words, or at least
disembodied expressions of love disguised
as chatter and sent to a disembodied love.

2.

So here I am in my usual pew, between
a supine Shakespeare – crapula must have struck –
and generous John Gower, gaudy as Blackpool Rock,
and stiffened flat, it seems, with atropine;
and slightly in front, the spastic lady's got a sticker
on her wheel chair: My Other Car's a Porsche.
She can read me: her senses are quicker
than ours, and she corkscrews at my applause –
which is entirely in my head.

is close to the distressed (I know) and she
can bless without trying, easily understands.
Tears embarrass my eyes: I have to see
through wet refractions our filtering blue host
astride the world like glass, with doves for hands.

3.
Outside the competers: competent and virtuous
(often ourselves); here – incompleteness; screening glass
chequered with flesh but letting stained light pass.
Worldliness to the rail – all words superfluous
and inexact, who hardly know what ails us.
That's why we're here. We're usually crass
or stony with good and evil, yet the Mass
invites the knower to be dubious.

It's our goodness and our knowledge he can't use:
they make us so benign – put in a class
apart. Clean with restraint, how messy if
we got crushy with love and played the silly ass!
Behind the unreadable fool the unspeakable hieroglyph –
and hermeneutics here would merely confuse.

4.
Insight is sousing in: grizzly mist on the horizon.
My sea's very upset: as if it can't
decide to ebb or flow – yet the sun's
quite tense, like a discus – or poised for a sprint
from cloudhole to cloudhole; rack hits salt, and
                                        everything
inside me tastes of brine – and there's so
surprising much it seeps over in tears, stinging
gladness, gratitude, unreadiness – sorrow!

182

Listening carefully to the sea – those huge hugs:
following its wriggling fingers, eeling down
and beckoning along drifting strata to the tug
of intense cold deep down below: shown
something quite different from anything you've seen before –
steering fishily up from an unknown floor.

5.
A week ago, what should I see but two young swans
who'd found each other; asleep in a ditch; full-grown
cygnets, brown on a green marsh mattress
of duckweed; dismantled wind-up gramophones . . .

Their beaks tucked back under a wing
like fold-up needle-heads – inward-bound,
as self-contained as two pies, till she felt me
looking and unsheathed her head, peeking around.

Then he woke too – quizzing more carefully,
solicitously, more protectively than she,
but, seeing no danger, turned a serpent's gaze
and studied her with deathless *agape*.

They considered sleeping again but felt a need
had come to paddle on; so, with slow care,
each tested the stretch of a brown wing
as if to know the gear was in repair –

and made two partings down the duckweed,
not parted in their partings. I had to know
swans love with inseparable love, and so our birdselves go
treading the water, not knowing on whom we feed.

6.
Shakespeare buried his actor brother
here, next to Massinger,
who neighbours Fletcher,
his honeyed collaborator
who might have lived longer
but for a septic delay
in plague-ridden London
to visit his tailor.

1607: Edmund Shakespeare:
just a year after
King Lear.
The sibling joke
about the bastard wicked brother
might make a brother choke
as he stood where we stand.
Those family names:
Hamnet died like Hamlet.

But Massinger, Fletcher, Shakespeare,
Henslowe and Alleyn,
men of this parish
who swashed and buckled for gain
have parted from their profits,
actorish or bearish,
and their names,
which we cherish,
their quibblings for King James,
and sprung to that perpetual spring
where no benumbing cold or scorching heat
can diminish anything
of what hangs here for ever
suspended in this air:
what men endure, the life of prayer.

Famine nor age have any being there.

7.

If the brain's the mind's rind
that we grip through the many senses, and striped wasps
sting and build as they do from a habit
they use like a pension, which works, though it keeps them
little machines, with genes for mastermind,

and man's the timeless but evolving kind, the least
grabbed by habit, copying, creating, hawking
new science and new solutions
that clock and alter his heart and will in time
draft how his body will officiate and feast,

not part goat, part ghost, but
an outward and visible cipher of an inward and spiritual
contriver, why does an old man polish brass
and peer from a door, as if for his life, wondering
why it never arrived, or trail his foot

past a funeral parlour that says 'We're here to help you'?

8.

Yes, you will smile, but does the mind exist,
the spook in this machine? But does the face –
broadly, that is, as we think it does, in space?
Looking at what we call a brain or fist,
who is it that perceives? Not that little cyst,
or camera, the eye: no actual image or embrace
pulses up the nerve tracks to race
the dendrites and tell you you've been kissed.

The brain is something we've imagined.
Our ganglia jerking, electricked
into ecstasy, who crooks this underpass
of input into insight? The flesh is grass,

an adoring face, or a twitching skin of conflict,
but who concocts these molecules into man?

9.
The hoisted leg and waddle of crows,
as if they'd no business with the grace
of birds – just a job to do,
eating, practical,
claws on the ground – except when they
lengthen out their finger-ended wings like hawks
and waft slow-flapping off
to another dung-heap.

                  These undertakers
seem so much closer to
men than a blackbird.

10.
I've forgotten the scruffy intellectual I once was.
Can I admit the divine man in friends,
in the hips of a camp Indian, in fag ends
of toothless tramps, washed policewomen, or the cross
in a class snub? It's my loss
that I'm one of the clean who condescends.
I scare the needy – my clothes can stink of dividends.

What God would want to know me? Though I'd like
to praise him, I stare out of a bay window
at a chirping garden, a holly tree, conker spikes,
a knowingness of late roses. They could imply
a mask of sorts: the passivity of this show
can blink like a face – everything in it an eye.

186

11.

The pelican hacks her breast and suckles with blood:
guilty pap of fledgelings of the good
who badly devour the edible breast – the musky silk
that circumvents with luxury our milk.
Wagner touched silk and cunt – smell and love of skin
that dies with love of death. The nectarine
and curious peach call up the ticklish nipple, even when
men prefer gardens. Yeats's famous interest
in death was but his longing for the breast
in Eden gone: he pressed and was impressed.
And how to let him out – the child inside
who knows no time, our nosy cause and guide:
love would disinherit him: he knows what's best.
Babies nurtured at their mother's breast
dream in unison with her, as if in the womb,
even when they sleep in a separate room.

12.

Innate science:
a martin inherits a technology
of clay pellets: a genetic testament.
Caspars don't build houses with their genes.
People learn what they can, repeat and imitate,
if pushed invent.

Words we have – almost like causes.
But a new elusiveness smiles
from our new names
which give us power to shake
the land that's barren now and cursed
for nomenclature's sake.

13.
Lionel Lockyer claimed his pills
had been distilled
from the rays of the sun:
they'd keep the agued carrying on
in fogs and the contagious air.

On his memorial bier
he seems to have a migraine
and a bicentenary grin
as one by one year after year
the tourists peer

at his well-wrought epitaph
and laugh.

14.
There's something we're always missing among
these antiquated people. They're strong
on only baring themselves to their personal sex.

They finger their thoughts by themselves,
with whisky bottles behind bookshelves,
and phantom touch, no fondling to perplex.

What could be fairer than their class
dues, but the upper upper are crass.
All kin are not brothers, or lovers.

At odds with bodies, they're cowed
by actual pricks and breasts, though proud
at mirrors, quick to see spots on others.

Find them attractive, and give them a hug, and they
rise to you, but quick – they pull away,
to bespatter you later out of rectitude.

Yearning for those shudders and delights,
they have to cope them in accepted rites
that prettify a calculating attitude.

One perfect intimacy: nothing else will do.
But it doesn't. The lies prick through,
and peccable sweet loving is subdued.

15.
Ave verum corpus: we're here – and halt –
because we're feebler than others, rock salt.
We limp with sclerosis, a stick for senile thighs,
an arm to help these lightweight brittle bones to rise –
and each audacious step a precipice
of hospitalization yet again: indignities –
flat feet, arthritic shuffle, sheer
ugliness, incontinence, smelliness or beer.

The first Adam was an advanced primate.
We creaking hairless gorillas malinger
to be cuddled, old dogs caressing our privates,
pressing our itching ears to kissing fingers.
Yet each has been called to be something else:
he calls us out from ourselves like funeral bells.

And the golden face looks out from the icon and glows,
supporting all this dole with God only knows.

16.
The lake crazes into splinters, jaggings, chips:
a wind like an artifice orchestrates the trees,
screams quietly, crescendos to a wheeze,
comes cracking down with thunder, lightning blips
and rain: a tremendous tutti, then diminuendo slips

squalling away. For ghostlier ears than these
a wind of no coming has knocked men to their knees,
rocking their standing with apocalypse.

My boat stops on a glassy lake, expects.
Light shines inside me vertically, thrown
through my head to the centre of the earth:
a husband comes inside through love, not worth –
face witnessing face and subject subject.
Amongst a world of glass who knows we're known?

17.
Hagar's in prayer – but breaks when the angel comes:
she didn't really expect it – or the sudden landscape
beyond the carnally twisting trees: how to escape
the non-molecular rock, the thumbs
on her ears, forcing her to look
at the river she knows she's got to cross,
that motionless boat, the fishers, the final fosse,
and the bridge weathering to original rock.

It crashes on her head – the great dismay:
no rules, no way,
no place to hide, and this that's just begun
now solider than the soil she's clung to. Pregnant today
but not with what she cannot bear, she spawns
in the desert a wild ass of a son.

18.
Oaks: nervous systems
against a December sky.
They tickle my dendrites
as my axons try
to escape infinity

for when I die
I'll feel vacuity
stretching like sky
and the tree of my body
left to lie
as I ask emptiness why
I lost identity
unless it was to try
as I do now
to rediscover entity
after pitching myself away
and learning to deny
in my hard way.

19.
This fly was born in this attic
with no food. What can he do but fuss,
plod up a pane of glass, fall,
buzz, plod up again like Sisyphus.
He was here yesterday, and the day before,
now he's got to the mullion, crawls
along it, round the corner, excelsior –
on a higher pane above. Outside, climatic –
all that the glass is blocking him from meeting.
I open the window. Retreating
upwards from the space above the sill,
he needs some coaxing with a pencil,
then side-slips into coldness that will kill.

20.
So here's the alarming silly tale again:
our father Abraham's call to murder a son,
hearing a voice – like the one near a Bradford grave
advising the Ripper to dekink casual love

with hammer, axe and sharpened tool,
to gouge and bash those girls just out of school.

And the father's needed sacrifice,
provision for a life, has had its price,
provision for a death. And for the son –
priapic expensive manhood's just begun.
So boys must learn of life on burning wickets:
rams caught by horns on convenient thickets.

Yet Abraham's caught by the horn – and aligns on the lie:
inwit, the great I Am, insights his eye.
We Israelites, the wandering heirs
of a bewildered dervish, are taught distrust in prayer.

21.
Brown in the autumn time, the grass is blown
and brittle, like a boy's hair
who's guessed, though not quite known despair.
Wind feels the bones of the wandering son
who whistles by the church, and the shuddering trees, down
by the slugsmeared arch, on some new scheme.
The viaduct drips and echoes on its stream,
flashing drops – printing a tune, then gone.

Alone, alone, it sings. The arch's echo
is a melody that somehow means to scare.
A train shrieks overhead, and he must go,
hooting and whistling too against the fear.
The lean wind grips him, twisting his curling hair.

22.
St Cuthbert's hopping – a cassock on the shore –
at two ravens rooting with their beaks
in the thatch he's heaved in the North Wind's roar
to top the hospice on the lonely island of Farne.
He can't believe their cheek.

'That's a *nest* you've got in your craw,'
he shouts, but the ravens scoff. 'In the name of Christ,'
he cries, 'it's for my friend, St Herbert! Yes, caw –
but come here again, and you'll get my boot, not straw!'
He's never been like this. They flap off fast.

Yet one comes back regardless. Cuthbert, bending to sow,
studies the trailing wings, reads what the crow will say.
Beak at feet, he bows, his croak is slow,
screwing his neck at Cuthbert and starting to go.
But Cuthbert catches his eye and grins: 'Well . . . stay.'

They both fly back, lugging a present of lard –
a gift you could grease your boots with. And by and by
he lets them live in his yard,
where they look askance at their saint – and doubly hard
at the hole he's built in the roof to watch the sky.

23.
All my most intimate talkers – they've been
men and women of inwit I never met:
survivors, inhalers, whom the threat
of the matter that matters or chore of citizen
compelled less than a whiff of ghostly oxygen
their nostrils flared at; Lawrence, Rilke, Herbert,
Wordsworth, Blake, Hopkins, Brontë, Dickinson:
abundant life's seductive martinets.

193

It's the whack
of the little beak that pecks the shell. Whiteness
glows through the crackable walls of the once big room
that's shrunk to a bag: one peck
and a great slit opens onto brightness.

24.
Now here's a cosy photo:
two seekers who look like fun –
both of them holding roses
and with curious costume on.
One is a mystical lama,
the other a lunatic don.
Both are bedragoned with visions
from *The Tibetan Book of the Dead*,
though the whole thing is loaded with dread
and may well have been once a con.
But something's gone right with the lama,
and something's gone wrong with the don.

25.
William Austin looked on his mother's face
and thought: As the clear light is upon the holy
candlesticks, so is the beauty of her face
in a ripe age. William was melancholy,
unsure about death, though he joyed in a well-writ book,
a picture and a song. No beautiful thing
is made by chance, he thought, but even of learning,
as of wine, a man may go on hungering
till it make him mad. Shall there be nothing
left me but the grave? Shall I at last
no other dwelling have? But till we come
to Thomas and his confession we have no Christ.

26.
All thoughts are parrots, pretty mocking birds.
Twitter about God's a cultural activity.
Does it show more than intertextuality
to shuffle packs of metaphysical absurds
or crap out concepts like a Luther's turds?
Reading the Bible's normal creativity:
the reader is the writer: each subjectivity
fabricates a Jesus from a text of words.

Your God's too human: those signifiers
were organized by stone-age Jeremiahs,
linguistically ingenuous desert bards . . .
which makes the Word a broadcast out of silence.
Intruded in the syntax, truth interlards
the structuring brain's concocted violence.

27.
To be sponged on
and neglected,
to have people take
and give cheek back
is, if you catch the joke,
to be godlike and grin sheepishly
as you sense the shepherd coming close.

It's in these silly
moments of blissful dying
that, elect with God
in your neglect,
you recognise the Host
and swallow without trying.

28.
'O God,' prayed Andrewes in secret every night,
'save me from making a God of the King.' To observe
the grass, herbs, corn, trees, cattle,
earth, waters, heavens, to contemplate
their orders, qualities, virtues, uses was
ever to him the greatest mirth, content
and recreation – held to his dying day.

Shakespeare had little Latin and less Greek,
while Lancelot had a lot of both, as well as
Hebrew, Chaldee, Syriack, Arabick, Aramaick.
'Your Majesty's bishop is a learned man
but he lacks unction: he rather plays with his text
than preaches it. Andrewes can pray as no
other man can pray, but he cannot preach.'

Yet if there were two saints of God in England
that summer, they were surely to be found
under the roof of the Bishop's Palace at Ely,
alone with their books and still at work with God –
abandoned souls – prostrate in the scholar's litany.
Casaubon and Lancelot Andrewes doubted they were
true scholars that came to speak to a man before noon.

'On the Real Presence we agree with the Romans;
our controversy is as to the mode of it.
We define nothing anxiously nor rashly.
There is a real change in the elements. But the death
on the Cross is absolute: all else is relative.
Christ is a sacrifice – so, to be slain.
A propitiatory sacrifice – so, to be eaten.'

But Privy Councillor to the royal pirate, fattening
his favourites? To dine at the court of flattery?
To be carried about, feasted and amused

by the heathen poor, who had to find for James,
Laud and Andrewes, horse, carriage, royal board
or feel the wrench of a rope around their neck?
And your Devotions slubbered and watered with penitent
                                                                    tears?

His Lordship kept Christmas all the year.
'Come and transfix a buck with me. I am
not well in my solitude: the hand that writes
these lines is ill with ague. Let me see
your dear face. If Stourbridge Fair, the finest
in England doesn't suit, I have beside me
a Matthew in Hebrew to make your mouth water.'

'A more servile and short-sighted body of men
than the bench of bishops under James the First never
set a royal house on the road to ruin.'
'Lord, I repent: help thou my impenitence.
Who am I, or what is my father's house,
that thou shouldest look upon such a
dead dog as I am. I spit in my own face.'

But who cursed the hanged and dismembered Gowries
every August before King James? At least
one commandment must have exceptions, as we're
the first to admit: our public executions
are marvels of technology in the Middle East
and help the Exchequer; the saintliest then
admitted the King's enemies should be hanged.

And so if persons nowadays feel squeamish
even about hanging, here at home, to say
nothing of drawing and quartering, it tells more
about the fashion of the age than about
an individual's virtue or conscience. Saintliness,
after all, is vicarious redemption, inviting grace,
not a capacity to see beyond your own time.

Andrewes prayed with dust on his head, a rope
around his neck: in great calamity we exercise
great devotion. A knighthood might be had
for sixty pounds, but only nothing will buy off
the irrefragable accusation of our lives.
Kings' benevolences are malevolences indeed.
But God hath not turned His mercy from our side.

29.
By the standards of Parliament
Jesus was very naive.
It's not that we're not all agreed.
We know what's rational,
it's that rationality's not compatible
with powerful interests and greed.

The world's very old,
much older than the Messiah.
And more modern.
The way things tread and science
between them
have trodden and trodden and trodden.

He didn't know
how the world wagged,
the politics of size.
To realize his ambitions
or even survive
he needed to compromise.

If he succeeded
in ruling the world
it'd have to be thanks
to the Roman Empire,
the Sanhedrin,
or nowadays the banks.

Unfortunately for him
he'd thought all this out
and got it wrong
in hallucinatory argument
with the Devil,
who loves the strong.

30.
On the cover of *Honest to God* there's a depressed
thinker. Perhaps all thinking is depressed.
It's depression that makes us think. Is it because
our faith's too cheerful that we miss sometimes the wit
only those who know the truth's always
absconding can hit? The Bishop's face
is blithesome and halcyon. To have faith in God,
even if 'God', perhaps, is not a word
we should use for a generation, is faith
in more than truth, for Jesting Pilate was inspired
to ask the question of the Way, the Truth and the Life.
The joke was on him, we presume. A reluctant revolution
is dying daily: difficult to admit
that what we know to be true is no longer true.
As we stand on our dung-heap of ideas and crow,
he slips away whispering 'I Am', to break bread
just when we're discussing his non-existence,
as we know from time to time but not in time.

And Bishop John Robinson left his scholarship,
waiting to see what he would learn from cancer.

199

31.
Elizabeth Newcomen once sold milk,
and Dorothy Applebee married a brewer.
The money in their legacies for beggars
and the schools they built
serialize immaterially
in children not yet born
and those who don't know where their luck comes from:
even goldener than the gilt
of Dorothy's candelabrum
still dangling like a rumour from the tower.

32.
The shark survives
although he doesn't chatter
like whales or major in science.
The quality of survival
doesn't matter.

We're pickled in our own solution.
The murders we watch on the box
we think we have to do.
History's watching beside us.
The skeleton that knocks
in the pipes is fossiled here inside us.

Is there a leap we're still not trying?
The dog that groans in travail on the floor
is waiting for me,
whimpering and sighing,
and feeling unspeakably more
not less than I,
as he twitches with loving fear.

I'm always saying goodbye.
He's always here.

33.
You who have bitten to the core
and cannot taste the apple
must stare in new confusion at your pain.
It's not enough to feel the ripple
of a twisted thigh within your brain –
you must feel more.

For those who tenderly built your prison
may split the walling skies to clear your sight,
and ecstasy that killed your crimson pleasure
reveal you newly walking, hair now bright,
the shocks of heavenly seizure
in the plains of beautiful light.

34.
We look for chocolate wrapped in silver paper
or Father Christmas, in from the planet Venus.
But he lives in sin and points to wounded feet
and hobbles round in distant labour camps
or dies unnoticed in a neighbouring street.
He whispers kindly when we start to eat him
and peeps at us from eyes of smelly tramps.

And, peeping back, we feel we're smelling death
and turn discreetly from distracting life.
His scripture is the dirt we're often doing.
He points our noses at our petty strife,
demands the loaves and fishes from our pockets –
provisions we're withholding from the war –
but adds to those who never feel accepted,

'Accept that you're accepted – as you are.'

35.
On the summit of St Thomas's Hospital
I felt no doubt. Easy to imagine
the buses and formicating cars
queuing for regroupment over Lambeth Bridge
were the last glints of a world I was leaving.

The Thames winked, and as the optical day
staged its illusory matinées of light,
the incredible stained to credibility:
God's love transferred from the pack
to man, dogging with joy and healing.

Infants who feel every passion
before they've felt the events
they won't understand when they happen
have the unwrinkled skin of those who
know the truth before they thrust
their hands in the slits of the bloody wounds.

36.
We meet again at the kneeling place
we plod to without emphasis,
where it's no disgrace
to face another face
as psychic invalids
with lowered eyelids.

In every lowered glance
we find provision
for the journey we're on.
Grace whispers grace
to his own face
through all these faces.

37.
Midnight Mass: Mervyn tells us
divinity desires a world like this burning tree.
The choir carols from every coign in turn
of the semi-darkened sanctuary,
tuning the stones
and topping them up with that plangent wine
the ghost mouth tastes in every graceful shrine.

I read the prayers from the lectern
and from all those bowed heads
an almost tangible breath has begun to flow;
my heart turns red
in the expanding now
and vertical as a chimney
I feel their flames go through me to the tower.

38.
Listening's dissolving. After I go –
surprise: I'm still here. I grasp for myself
and find myself ungraspable. I know
me, but I eludes me. I am
is the person I've just been, inside my head.

I am in endless space, aware
of watching as I'm watched. The me is a bugged cell
with a one-way mirror, surrounded by everywhere.
I see the bright screen in the dark, but power failure
reminds me of the emptiness where I am.

39.
Dear God, as I sweat around the park for death,
I think with every bronchial breath

I'm running for life. Slow progress makes the track
seem seamless. But we know it was only the crack
of comminating thunder, thrashing through flashes
in crashing streets, with no friend or hope of sanity,
no love, no hope, no charity,
that made me see my faces turning to ashes.

We need our deaths to make new tracks. The black
doors grieve open and we see an Easter Day
breaking like spring – your remarkable way
of coming to meet us in your Mass,
making us see through wine as if through glass.

40.
Whisky's a risky aspect of the Body:
a distilled divine. All sacraments are risky.
Ecstasy can booze you to the devil –
the Dog of God: *Deus est diabolus
inversus*: the Hounds both hunt the world
as a team (see *Job*) and often it's the Dog who pads
with the prey to God. Whisky killed my dear
old dad and that's what drove my mother mad.
Death's certainly the alcoholic's mother:
those first erotic bubblings at the bottle
or breast are gaspings of our love of Her
or Him or Both, all Three, met shuddering as we rattle.
How long will it be before we find Cockayne
where the whisky rivers flow, so stilly flow,
like every poison from the flesh of God,
with peaty water, heart of gold, an amber glow?

41.
Imbecile to the wise and sane, our baby divination
is milky eyes staring at bosoms to be hugged

not clouded in concepts: an infinite sky's plugged
into an infant's irises of contemplation.
Impatience
at lugging Moses' stones is right:
the yoke must be easy, the burden light.

The lost are often first.
Sprinting from God
they won't be coerced.
They see him at the winning post,
give way to a crush,
and fall like fools while the prudent only plod.

42.
I hardly ever meet my brothers and sisters.
Here perhaps on holy ground
is the proper place.
But what we pass around
is the shining handshake, called the kiss of peace.

What can I do but intercede for the publicans
and drinkers, not here, but my actual friends?
There must be, I suppose, quite special roles
for every Madeleine. Who knows what He intends?
And is the kiss impetuous in cautious souls?

My cronies are didactic: one showed me
a film of far more breathless peaceful kisses:
'These rather lovely girls and ugly chaps'
had overcome the prejudices
'that make us buy these films and watch perhaps.'

They seem to be quite enjoying what they're paid for,
so prodigal and naughty with caresses;
but surely it's the Producer
who asks for tender smiles and licking kisses
and makes each woman long for her seducer?

43.
'Bore men if you must,
but must you bore God too?'
demands Isaiah:
Mervyn's maiden text
to fluff the dust,
knowing it might backfire.

Or take a homeless pair
out of the fifty thousand,
and their baby, and an ass,
to construct a living crib
in Trafalgar Square.
The plods on the beat don't like it.
Nor do the brass.

'We've got a crib already –
next to the tree . . . and hark!
The carols are starting up
on St Martin's steps.'
Mervyn and Trevor plod
with mitre, crook and nod
to a legal plot in the park,
a nook where no one'll see
their demythologizing cot but God.

44.
Of hem, that written us to-fore
John Gower is erst in loves lore.
Tho he be dede and elles were
We thenken on his presens her,
Tho other worde of hem nought is,
Aperte fro thet he writen has,
Then mariage lisens and his wille
And tomb that stondeth to us stille.
A squere he was and born in Wales
And wened it gode writen in tales
Somewhat of lust, somewhat of lore,
Tho loves lust and lockes hore
In chambre accorden never more,
And leved he in time of blody kinges
And civil warres and tresons swinges.
But Gowerlond, tho fond in Wales,
More sothely is a lond of tales.
Ther ben also that seyn he was
In Yorkshire born from Conquerors,
And otheres seyn in argument
That he was born and bred in Kent,
But as a Suffolk man minself,
Tho adopted so, boghten in by pelf,
I wene he was a Suffolk man,
That leved in Multon manor a span,
And atte leste hadde frends in Kent
And eke therto establishment.
Dan Chaucer was his poete frend,
A yonge prentice, of hem ytrened.
He preies for Charite, Merce and Pite –
Kindenesse herd to finde in a cite –
His hair hath roses intertwined
With ivy – tribute to his minde
Versed both in bokes and science,
Of which he made an holy alliance.

But Godes curse had yfallen on
His lond in great confusioun.
He wended out to gathre flowres –
Insted he sawe a lond of hores
Chaunging into forme of bestes:
Swine in the cite atte theyr festes,
Assess weninge they weren horses,
Dogges that licked the children's sauces,
Oxen proude of dragones tailes,
Venus lost in a lond of wailes,
And so his *Liber Amoris* sholde be
On how men moten love joiesle.
Swanne at his necke, at his fete a lion,
His sawle hath victore oer angeres scion.
Preie for his sawle, and as your guerdon
He boghte thusand dayes of perdon.

45.
My chest crackles with bronchitis –
and I ask myself, What is it then in me
that's so unhappy with the air?
Air: it goes to my blood, it's everywhere,
it's deeply intimate with my terminal skin.
Cloud teashops, lakes of anodyne,
they float up there,
and here
her breast and her vagina –
the air's been teaching how to breathe them in.
My lungs are touch, the kiss of the eye still finer.

Enclosed in stone, I breathe through stone like skin.
The cathedral's ribs and groins
can splice me to all space –
another air and psychic terrain
extended by the cinematic brain,
sustained by grace.

208

46.
When I was thirty-two I got cancer:
probably a proxy for something else,
but it took me by surprise. Time was unhurried
in the specialist's ante-room. To me it seemed
clouded with witnessing comforters. I imagined nuns
spilling their love in prayer for the sick and worried.

The specialist ogled it through a tiny lens
like one I'd had at school. He didn't think
it was cancer. Better to have it off, though. No
innuendo – but doubtless truth in that.
Two weeks later I'm taut on a clinical table,
waiting for stitches out and ready to go.

A houseman came in first in a pure white coat,
with high heels, and leaned against a wall,
hands folded behind his bum. His smoky eyes
were observant I knew to see how I would take it.
The specialist bustled in, with a hand-wag,
assuringly: 'It was cancer.' No surprise.

He'd examined every cell. There was healthy flesh
all the way round. The nurse was looking embarrassed.
Who'd not heard of people cured of the dread
disease, and only a year later – they're dead?
Melanoma, a beautiful name for a fast,
distorting and painful killer when it spreads.

So I needed a little treatment: 'belt and braces.'
Regular visits for radium: massacre the cells
in case a wild one escaped. And so I rubbed
shoulders with the dead and dying. I remember a lady
carefully lipsticking lips before a mirror.
My reprieve could make me somehow feel quite snubbed.

The scar will always be mine: it makes me nervous
with women: not gold, but the size of a silver guinea –
and a wound in the side – but the other side from Christ's.
It'd be rather fun to lie: a piece of shrapnel
got me here, instead of my cushy war.
It looks like a brand on a pig about to be priced.

It only exists in my mind. I conned a surgeon
to carve it out – to leave merely a long
white scalpel line like a sabre wound.
On the beach it won't raise questions: more discreet.
I remember a friend in a pub and remember thinking:
'He'll be kissing the girls when I'm long underground.'

Dead now. I'm here but in his club.

47.
Somewhere there's a man who took me fishing
and kept me sane. I don't even
remember his name. Stephen . . .
some saint's name: unintellectual, observant, well-wishing.

This useless work has risks. Near to splitting,
Rilke thought his grit in loneliness came
from glassy evenings on Capri, all the same,
with two old dears, in a deck chair, watching them
                                        knitting.

One of them sometimes had an apple to pass.
A tiny ugly dog with sorely swelling boobs
craved for his eyes in its solitude. The sugar cube
he gave her was a wafer in a private Mass.

48.
Perhaps those childish ecstasies of terror
when midnight pulsed on midnights of blind hate
and vampires hung behind the stirring curtains
alert for children's eyes to close and sleep
were deaths we might have had or can anticipate.
How we need to have an expert mother
to sit beside us, spreading unconcern,
and mock the terminal illness in the corridor
and tell us that it's not our turn:
the custom-built disease has gone next door.

Perhaps in every aged impotent craving
the child we were is still inside us, crying
for a rocking knee, and not believing
what we heard can never be,
though finding mother's presence near the sea:
to feel the lift from fifty fathoms
and know annihilating pleasure
of sea absorbing self in sea,
far greater than the logic
of non-acceptance on the certain shore.

49.
Some day I'm going to have to meet my mother
again. I'm not sure how it will be.
Will she be splashing that arctic fox she wore
for the sepia studio plate they had of us three
a month or two after my birth? I must feel kin
with those still girlish eyes and lenient lips –
pleased, my father proud. I'd find her smooth skin
and neck attractive, her kind intelligent hips
seductive, her Parisian costume and pearls, and her
silky hat all that could make a baby purr.

I can hardly pray for her soul. I feel meagre
because she died before she died,
too soon for me, and recouped as one too eager
and helpless to help, in need herself. I sighed
for an intellectual love, all nous
without the feeling. I gave her the best books
to read; she read them greedily. It was
too late. The lesion had been scored. The crux
now was: survival meant to disregard
the conscience she gave and find a new mother instead.

November, the month of holy souls. I'd like
to feel gratefully for those first baths,
her cherishing hands on my skin, those grey eyes
so tender even in my stubborn wraths,
my baby safety under it all. But misgiving
had made her need me more than I needed her,
and what I feared most was her fear of living.
The day she found us infant boys and girls
exploring bums in the bathroom was the worst.
She wouldn't speak, and both of us felt cursed.

No, the worst . . . Yet is she listening now? Who else
could understand her like her only son?
And who could understand me like herself?
She knew me even if her mind went wrong.
She wished me well, though neither of us knew
the way to the other's happiness. Surely now,
sophisticated in another life, she can review
more expertly than I. She must know how
to nurse me to myself when I too leave behind
all the crazy blocks that pave my mind.

I'll need some friends who've been there when I go.
As my breath scratches the last scribbles, and I write

212

'The End', letting go of everything I know,
I'll need a helping hand in those streets of light.
Can anyone love the glaucous eyes of weakness?
Though I've got through life with the back of my head
turned to most neighbours, trusting in obliqueness,
the mother will lean one night by the cot of dread
for my sensible eyes to close in sedative calm
and the moment when I perceive who I really am.

50.
There's no abiding city here.
A gentleman's
enfranchised everywhere.
But being at home everywhere
is to be at home nowhere.

The Son of man hath not where
to lay his head.
Even the dead
have laid their heads
where they're not.

We've had far to go
and have farther.
There's no emptiness
like where home was,
and it won't get less.

In the tale the prodigal son
staggers back home
and sees his father running.
We've gone farther –
we're not who we were.

Our Father's stranger too, no longer
in that Old Folks' Home.
We might not recognize him –
or, shocked, try to revise him,
perhaps disguise him?

To meet an old friend
after forty years
is to know, though
that what you've lost in going
doesn't go.

51.
People that swim clambered
onto the land.
Fins elevated into wings
and became the *status quo*
for excitable birds.
The tiny ampersand
that was crouching on to man
had far to go.

My patriarch was a man
called Australopithecus.
He bounced inside his gland
the sperm that quickens us.
And did he have a soul?
Or when the angels scanned
the daughters of men
and saw that they were beautiful
did something non-indigenous
scintillate inside that skull?

When One had made it all he saw
it was beautiful and true and good.

Adam's law
has split us into two.
And was the tree
that fruited on the spine
of Neolithic or Cro-Magnon man
a breaking awareness of a larger brain,
or was it law
to help the ploughman to retain
the bread his sweating brow
had toiled to win?

Round good and evil
winds the Devil,
our Accuser
with gifts of clothes
and the *felix culpa*,
trading lust for love,
with loss of Eden, all our woe,
and Cain's
war for grain.

Since Satan's a lawyer
and a gentleman judge
how can he tolerate
that the first Adam,
a stone-pitching primate,
can be the second
in a Paradise
of forgiven vice?

Through the gate
the Scandalous Word
conducts each malefactor:
past the flaming sword
and the elder brother
with his unprodigal grudge.

Unfair –
the love that makes
the lost and last the heir:
last here, first there,
inheriting without merit
an Eden of brotherhood
and incompetence for good.

Beyond the scenery
the in-itself
and its particular machinery
still elude us. But
whatever everything is
it still includes us,
eyeless creatures prodding
at an elephant's toe,
or a foetus in the amniotic fluid,
listening to a mother's radio.

Mother science is
the prodigal one
the Father welcomes in
with healing and revealing
learned studying among husks,
finding in the musk of swine,
especially there,
the absconded divine.

If moments occur
when eyelids seem to open,
eyes even then
have to learn vision.
These overarching arches are
the womb of Mary.
We look towards the hymen,
the eastern light

stained blue like sky
or blue like Mary
against the particular night.

52.
Invisible reader, impossible God,
there are times we dream you back to being
an irascible blustering Yahweh, haranguing
a gang of bedouin, but not too often.
I try to listen to your presence
quietly as an astronomer, an absence in the
                                    room,
the mother and father I imagined in the dark
when I was sick, who never came.
You're the pebble on the beach with spread
arms and a navel, the fearful passage
past the graveyard, a thorn in the flesh,
the psychiatrist who buggered off while
                                    listening,
yet in spite of everything somehow managing
to see me too in my deliberate vanishing.

XI

. . . we must be in some way four-dimensional, if we understand that man and the universe cannot be taken separately.
– Maurice Nicoll, *Living Time*

VISITATIONS

1. *The Child*

At midnight I go down to the lake
and sit watching light on the water.

It's stained glass: greens,
reds and blues hang in the trees.

A naked child emerges
perfectly-grown, a foetus,

navelstring and placenta
still in place, dangling.

Ignoring me, it walks the bank
and turns, to sit watching the lake.

I sit beside it, hoping it'll speak to me,
at least acknowledge my existence and presence.

But it belongs elsewhere.
I say, 'I'm sorry.'

It looks reproachfully at me, then smiles,
and floats back into the lake.

First it seems to be swimming,
then it slowly disappears,

creasing and smoothing the surface,
like an aquatic creature.

2. *The Face*
The face pressed to my bedroom window
is only a face. It slides into my room,
flops onto the floor,

and its black hair and eyes are full
of tender longing. It creeps into bed with me
and cuddles, slimy and rather smelly.

I feel very uncomfortable: it's so alien,
slimy and rather smelly and,
being very sensitive, it notices.

I apologise and say
I can't help being human,
it's in my genes.

Sensitive, it slides
out of bed and under the bed
and finds a chamber pot.

It drinks the pee and turns beautiful woman,
climbs into bed with me, and I'm
strangely comfortable with her

even though I know she's
really a black slimy thing
that came out of the night.

3. *The Man*
When I open the door
the same man's there,
in his trilby.

He pushes by, walks upstairs
and sits down in the drawing room
in his coat and hat.

He still has no face and, when he
takes his coat and hat off,
under his double-breasted suit he's invisible.

I sit down opposite and wait for him to speak.
After a while he says,
'I'm waiting for you to speak.'

I say, 'I can only speak to myself.
That's why I'm here
and you're not.'

He gets up silently
and disappears, leaving
his coat and hat on the chair.

DESPATCHES

for V.S.

1.
Does he still walk
Piccadilly with
the white flash in his cap?

I see myself driving
these eager streets
as the one that vanished might:

a remote trajectory,
beyond kin
and comprehension.

2.
I look her name up
and it's in the directory.
Surname. Initial. Hers?

Spectres of spectres
who sat in the flesh
at Gielgud's *Hamlet*,

we were ghostlier
than the Ghost:
the silence and watch

of eternal love
in transient bliss
with the taste of an afterlife:

224

all that violence
our spectacular paradise,
Hamlet being ourselves.

3.
Later,
in a salad restaurant,
it's lettuce, lights, smiles.

Forgetting passing-time
we outstay
our curfew!

Outside, in blackout
and explosions, she knows
a certain window,

and, for me,
unbelievably,
the sentry's off for a pee!

I tiptoe upstairs in boots
in my Baker Street billet,
able to see her again.

And two years later,
when I call at her barrack,
she's gone.

4.
Time brings
absence. Demobilized,
we walk as exiles

in unspeakable history
from unspeakable childhood
and the invisible partner.

Queer inked-over photographs,
thinking we're living
the lives we're living,

we didn't exist, except
'one enchanted evening
across a crowded floor',

putting our truly great trust
in gas and dust and mist
and the invisible partner.

5.
Name in a telephone book,
who was the girl in the khaki skirt
and forties hair still haunting

a blacked-out street,
a lighted club,
and a life we never went to bed with?

FAUSTUS SPEAKS

pecca fortiter, sed fortius fide . . .
. . . sin boldly but believe boldlier . . .
      – Martin Luther

1. *Purple Heron*
Suddenly it's there –
before we know it –
the purple heron.

It sits by the reeds,
neck erect, not necessarily
watching, but listening.

A bird's always alert,
with that impersonal
ruthless eye,

feeding and mating,
tender with the young,
obeying the laws of God.

What law do we follow
when illicitly we find
we love each other?

Isn't illicitness
somehow more generous
than possession?

So many in matrimony
are asunder, not
joined together by God.

227

2. *Faustus Today*
My car radio's playing Liszt's Mephisto waltz
with diabolical tritones, then Dutch baroque music,
then Liszt's fantasia on *Don Giovanni*.

Liszt is one of my presiding spirits.
Only the fantasia's wide of the mark.
Anyway, even if I'm dancing to the

alluring music of youth, you're no Gretchen.
Sophisticated, intelligent, witty, humorous,
you know what you want and what you're about.

Here's two on's are sophisticated. Alive,
though, with the old unsophisticated sigh:
'I want to love and be loved!'

It's not so easy to be loved, though, is it?

3. *Fly*
Is every fly
an emissary
of Beelzebub?

They vomit on your food
then stomp on it
to suck up the juicy pulp.

Whenever there's
one fly in the room
there are two of you.

It's not certain who's
more important in God's eyes
or Beelzebub's.

The fly has skills:
walking upside down,
flying sideways,

avoiding swipes,
knowing when it's
snack or mealtime.

When will we learn
to accept our blackness
and the buzz of our black hearts?

4. *Passionate Friendship*
Since what we have
after a false start
is a passionate friendship,

I've understood
how far we are
from where we started.

Do I see in you
the integrity
I've lost?

Do I see in me
the integrity
you haven't found?

It seems a pity
to spend a whole
lifetime becoming

a candidate for Hell,
but we grow
and we grow corrupt.

And corruption
is the compost
growth grows in.

5. *Sunflowers*
I stare at a V-sign: sunflowers
fallen off a barge
on a canal at Amsterdam.

I read the entrails:
yellow petals
with an umber heart.

Just as I, speaking,
don't always allow
for your swiftness

you, in your presentation,
may not have allowed
for your audience's slowness.

But if they don't grasp
your point or your pun
they'll grasp your brilliance.

It's raining.
The sun's out of sight
but no less brilliant.

Then, in the evening,
I'm getting slightly drunk
on duty-free Black Label.

There's a distant piano.
I'm weary of time and
counting the steps of the sun.

When I'm dead and you're
famous, perhaps I'll be watching
from behind the sun

or beyond the sun,
counting your steps.
Perhaps I'll be younger than you.

6. *The Purple Heron Again*
Growing old, the phoenix
sees a girl like a funeral pyre
and, turning body to sun,

burns himself out,
rising from his ashes
nine days later.

In Heliopolis
the hieroglyph for sun worship
is a heron-like bird.

The sun dies in his own fires
nightly, and every morning
rises again from Egypt.

Life is the
ritual sacrifice
of a purple heron.

7. *Earthly Paradise*
I lived alone, feeding on
light from the stars.

At the end of a thousand years,
knowing death was nearing,

I descended to Phoenicia and built
a nest of spices in the tallest palm.

At dawn, lifting my voice,
I sang a hymn so beautiful

I knew I was a poet and, that instant,
the rising sun stood still.

Sparks from its flames lit on my nest.
Instantly I rose from the ashes,

lifted up the aromatic dust
and flew to Heliopolis.

I placed the ash on the sun temple altar
and winged towards my distant Paradise.

Thousands of birds followed me,
in friendship, singing.

8. *Why He Wants to go to Bed with Her*
You want to know,
Did I want to go to bed with you,
and was that why I liked your poetry?

No: I watched and heard you
reading your poetry

and I loved you and feared you.

I wanted to go to bed with you
to overcome my fear. When love is
become perfect, it casteth out fear.

Would I have loved you if you were fifty?
How can I answer a question like that?
What I do know and can tell you is this:

I feel a lot safer with women in their fifties.

9. *The Healer*
You yawn with that little
owl-like hoot that's so charming.

Or your eye criticizes
your look in the hotel mirror.

Are you dressed avant-gardedly enough
for a conference on the connected body?

You're perfect: just yourself,
as if your mind had clothes on.

I can see you're turning healer,
and I the child.

I'm decades too late
to be the lover you deserve.

As you sense my insecurity
you become more secure.

Perhaps my weakness
is given to help you.

But to help you to what?
Am I becoming your mouse?

10. *Bells*
Cracked bells ring the St Anthony Chorale
before twelve deep notes.

One, you don't love me.

Two, you seem to need me.

Three, you only think you need me.

Four, sex is easy for you.

Five, you gave it because you needed me.

Six, if sex would have made you lose me,
you'd have withheld it.

Seven, your security about sex
makes me insecure about sex.

Eight, your feeling of the unimportance of sex
is incomprehensible to me.

Nine, if it's unimportant,
why are you withholding it?

Ten, for me sex is love,
and that makes it difficult.

Eleven, for you sex is not love,
and that makes it easy.

Twelve, what is it that's
brought us together?

In the dark silence I wonder,
Why do we want to talk to each other?

11. *Redemption*
Profane as we are, poets must,
like St Paul or St Augustine,

tell what goes on in us
against all reason and morality.

So we both bring our best and worst
to our love, and our love

wrecks the journey, displaying us crudely
one to another, to ourselves.

Near Ghent there's a fire on the line.
We change trains and miss the ship.

Later at night, we entrain for Victoria
and a man is killed under us on the line.

The tube from Brixton announces
Victoria is closed: the fire brigade's there.

In the small hours we taxi to a coach station.
Later I ring, exhausted, frustrated and drunk.

I rang to see if you'd arrived safely,
but I scare you with my paranoia.

12. *Skin*
An inflammation on the skin
can be a sign of sin –

not sin done,
but sin undone –

some act of love,
licit or illicit –

immoral grace
in the place

where fingers
ought to visit.

13. *Sehnsucht*
Yearning's better in a foreign language:
the word obliterates that look of familiarity.

Sehnsucht's an agony stronger than sex
only assuageable by the connected body.

Have you any idea how precious
your bits of paper are to me?

For you, hasty missives,
dashed off to save a letter,

for me, presences of inadequate handwriting,
standing in for the presence I long for.

The agony of being alive is so strong
nothing can assuage it except your body.

Sehnsucht's an elongated agony
parallel to eternity and going on for ever.

14. *The End*
It was sad to see your sheets
revolving in the washing machine.

I shan't forget your breath
coming rhythmically on my shoulder

and your breath on my mouth
while you were asleep.

It's a privilege to know you're prettier
with your clothes off than on,

which isn't true of everyone.
I know where your moles are,

what your toes are like
and I love your teeth

and your long nose.
I know how sweetly you smell.

There are moments when I can
look right through your hazel eyes

to the person looking out.
Our eyes are in touch with

transcendence. Some day
shall we be together?

'Earthly Paradise' is indebted to ANIMALS OF THE
IMAGINATION AND THE BESTIARY by Thetis Blacker and Jane
Geddes, The Prince of Hesse and the Rhine Memorial Lecture, 1994.

238